PLAYING
PRO FOOTBALL
TO WIN

PLAYING
PRO FOOTBALL
TO WIN

by JOHN UNITAS
with HAROLD ROSENTHAL

Foreword by Carroll Rosenbloom

DOUBLEDAY & COMPANY, INC., GARDEN CITY, NEW YORK

Library of Congress Catalog Card Number 68–25598
Copyright © 1968 by John Unitas and Harold Rosenthal
All Rights Reserved
Printed in the United States of America
First Edition

CONTENTS

Johnny Unitas doesn't need me, or anyone else, to beat the drums for him as the greatest quarterback the game has known. The record does this, in eloquent fashion. He has completed more passes, rolled up more yardage, and thrown more touchdowns than anyone in the half-century history of pro football.

Neither Johnny nor I have been around that long. His first year with the club—the only club for which he has ever competed in the major leagues—was 1956. It was a year I remember well, because for the first time we began to permit ourselves the luxury of thinking we had a chance to go all the way. Students of football history will recall that the Colts didn't quite set the world afire at the start.

At the beginning of the 1956 season our regular quarterback was George Shaw. In the fourth game he was hurt against the Chicago Bears. That gave Johnny his chance, and off his losing performance that day no one would ever have dreamed that he was tomorrow's superstar.

He was extremely downcast after the game, and I felt he needed some words of encouragement. I've never seen a first-year player who couldn't use some. As I stopped in front of his locker, I said, "Johnny, forget what happened today. Just remember, you're going to be a great one."

A good many years have passed since, so I'm hurting no
one by recalling that there was more than a suspicion of
tears in his eyes. "Boss," he said, "I hope so."

In a dozen years Johnny Unitas became not just one of
the "great ones," but "the greatest."

It's difficult to recall his best game, although I suppose
you'd have to pick the title playoff of 1958 against the
Giants. Most football people feel that the sport's tremendous boom in the past decade started right there in that
overtime classic. Oh, it would have come anyway, but the
Colts' dramatic victory made it happen just a little sooner.

I think 1958 was Johnny's most dramatic year in many
ways. He had gone through twenty or so games with a
touchdown or more in every game when he was hurt early
in a game against Green Bay. He was hurt badly. A rib
had punctured his lung and it's doubtful whether he got
more than a few minutes of sleep a night for the next
couple of weeks.

That's how long he stayed out, however; just a couple
of weeks. He was back for the game with the Rams, and
while all of us sat biting our nails, wondering what would
happen if he took a bad wallop on the wrong side, Johnny
calmly stepped back on the first play and threw a fifty-
eight-yard bomb to Lenny Moore. Los Angeles never recovered from that initial six-pointer and we won a big victory, 34–7. How rusty can you really get in two weeks?

To help him play so soon after he was injured the trainer
devised a protective device for John to wear. It was at-
tached to his shoulder pads, came down in front, and went
around to his back. It was heavy and bulky, and you wondered how he could even raise his arms, much less throw
with that pinpoint accuracy of his. We all watched a little
nervously as he tried it for the first time. "How is it,
Johnny?" we asked.

His answer was a simple, "I can throw with it."

For the balance of the season he wore the contraption. And he wore it in the championship playoff, though this was something few people realized, certainly not the general public. It was the greatest demonstration of courage I ever saw in football.

Most of us don't keep ten-year-old figures in our heads. Fortunately, Johnny's new book offers for the first time a record of the forty-seven-game streak in which he threw one or more TDs a game. This is one of the really great records in sports. It ran from December 9, 1956 through December 4, 1960, and it spanned five seasons. It provided five million thrills.

Any attempt to describe Johnny's character, his consideration for others, his dedication, would take up a considerable amount of space in a book which must place a premium on such space. Let me put it this way:

No player in pro football has ever been held in higher regard by his teammates. They have always been aware of his intense desire to win, but always as a team player. He has consistently put this ahead of all thoughts of personal records and achievements. Rightly, they look to Johnny Unitas as their leader.

Johnny Unitas started as a Colts' player and he'll finish as a Colts' player. When he does, it is my hope that he'll be a member of the Colts' official family forever.

Carroll Rosenbloom
PRESIDENT, BALTIMORE COLTS

1. View from the Passing Pocket

It's very easy to sound like an expert in discussions of pro football, especially if you stick to criticisms of quarterback styles. You separate all signal-callers into two classes: those who stay in the pocket and those who don't. You take a deep breath and announce (if you are talking about a quarterback who will "roll out" or "scramble"), "No one has ever won a championship with a quarterback who didn't stay in the pocket."

And you'll be right, because no one has. But that doesn't make you right next year, or the year after that because someone has to come along, break all the rules, and still be a winner.

Actually, what staying in the pocket really does, in addition to giving you the maximum amount of protection from your blockers, is provide you with an opportunity to throw the ball between the gaps.

What are the gaps? They represent the spacing between the rival linemen.

First, let's look at size in the game today. We like a quarterback to be six-three or six-four, if possible, because the size of the linemen has increased. I'm six-one, and 196 pounds. I think a fellow six feet can do the job. Anyone smaller has a big disadvantage.

A lot depends on what type of people a quarterback has playing with him. After all, there's no one who can throw the ball sitting on the seat of his pants all day.

A quarterback has to have time to throw the ball. And he has to know where it is going.

The secret of an effective offensive line is keeping a good split. This causes the defensive linemen to split, too, because they must shift to cover their men. Natural gaps are thus created, and this is where you throw the ball—in the gaps. Start throwing over the heads of the players in front of you and you'll find yourself in more kinds of trouble than you ever thought possible.

Ideally, to split the defense, we like to have the guard two or three yards away from the center and the tackle about the same distance from the guard. This forces the defensive lineman to play head-up on your offensive line.

Occasionally your offensive linemen will get beat to the inside. They will then tend to close the gap down in order to give the defensive linemen only one way to go. When this happens, the quarterback is robbed of his gap and it's like throwing up against a solid wall. After a few times you have to do a little strong talking in the huddle.

Speaking of huddles, I've always called all the plays. Not that I don't consult with Don Shula and the other coaches on the sideline when the opposing team has the ball, just as I consulted with Weeb Ewbank when he ran the Baltimore club. But it has always been left to me to decide what play was to be run. Of course the punting situations and the field goal attempts are matters of coaching strategy, but the rest is mine. I have to take the credit— or the rap for it.

Of course, you have to go with the personnel at your

command, and you can't ever ask them to execute beyond their abilities. Maybe some other club is winning big
with passing in a particular season, but before you start
trying to imitate them, make sure you have the passer *and*
the receivers. And when you think it's a good idea to mix
up your offense, showing them a bit of a power play off
tackle when they're looking for the pass, make darned
sure you have the runners *and* blockers who can make
that play go for you.

The big thing is execution. It doesn't make any difference how many plays you have, or how many plays you
are able to run. They aren't any good unless you can make
them work, and only the right personnel can do this.

You get the personnel mainly from the annual draft, that
is the new personnel, which has to be kept coming all the
time because football teams grow old and wear out just
like everything else. With twenty-six pro clubs in the
majors now, and more on the way, it's getting increasingly
difficult to come up with the particular player you want,
especially if you've finished reasonably high the year before
and consequently are picking far down the line. What most
talent departments do today is to set up two prime picks,
first the man they want most for some particular job,
and secondly the man they rate the best football player
available, regardless of position.

That gives them two choices. If they're lucky they'll
come up with one by the time it's their turn. Computerized
talent evaluation has made it extremely difficult to pick
"sleepers" the way some of the clubs have done in the
past. Raymond Berry, the Colts' great receiver, was a
twentieth-round "future" pick back in 1954. Around the
same time, Rosey Brown, the Giants' perennial all-pro
offensive tackle and now a Giant line coach, was a twenty-
seventh-round pick out of a newspaper clipping. Today's

computers would have blown a fuse, solid-state tran-
sistors or not, frantically signaling, "Tilt."

I'm a pocket passer, although I might do a little more
running than most. Not that I lie awake nights looking
forward to running with the ball. It's merely that sometimes such extreme measures are necessary. My most serious
injuries haven't come while I was running with the ball,
though they have occurred in standard passing situations
where the pass blocking has broken down or some defending blitzer has gotten lucky.

In 1967 one of the records I eclipsed was Y. A. Tittle's
lifetime touchdown mark. He had finished up with 232
and a deserved reputation of being one of the really exceptional pocket passers.

Y.A. liked to throw the ball off play-action passes. He
had great backs to work with when he was in San Francisco, men like Hugh McElhenny, and Joe Perry, who set
rushing records in the era before Jim Brown. I sometimes
wonder why they never won the championship or even the
conference crown, but maybe the West was always the
tougher section in which to win.

Y.A. is still very much in football, coaching the 49ers'
quarterbacks. When he was playing, he was a superb faker.
He could hide the ball extremely well, sticking it on his
hip, or tucking it into his body. He was simply great on
the bootleg play, although he was almost destroyed during
one of these maneuvers against us in Baltimore in the opening game of 1963.

That was a tough game for New York, the club with
which Y.A. was to finish his career the following year.
We had them 28–24 at the half. They wanted to catch
up badly, and in their first drive they encountered a couple
of frustrating obstacles. First Y.A. got off a dandy pass from
midfield to Del Shofner, who caught it on the twenty-five

and would have gone all the way if he hadn't gotten tangled up with the field judge on the four-yard line.

The player always loses in that situation. It's up to him to keep from making contact with the officials, who are presumed to be trying to do the same thing.

So there they were on the four when an offside penalty put them back on the nine. Then Tittle missed with a pass to Frank Gifford, and by this time he decided he was through allowing the hired help to mess things up. He "bootlegged" the ball the rest of the way and he got it across the goal line. But there our cornerback, Lenny Lyles, made one of the most unusual smashing tackles I've seen.

Tittle had his head down, and as he scored he crashed into Lyles' shoulder pads. His head was jammed between his shoulders and he was through for the day. That night an ambulance met the Giants when they got off the train in New York, and Tittle spent the night in the hospital. He raised a fuss about riding in the ambulance, though, and finally settled for sitting up front with the driver.

When Tittle missed the following week's game, which the Giants lost 32–0 in Pittsburgh, it appeared that he and the Giants were through for the year. But Y.A. did come back and he did lead the Giants into the playoff against the Bears.

Tittle's style was a little different from most. He passed with a three-quarters motion. I guess you'd have to call him a side-armer more than anything else. His long passes were very accurate. He wasn't the fastest quarterback in the world, but he was still quick in his late years. A man may be slow getting from one place to another, but he can still get a good jump with his first two or three steps, and that was Y.A. Actually, I'd rate quickness more important than speed in a quarterback.

When a quarterback goes back to set up he has to get there in the shortest amount of time possible. I like to put seven to ten yards between myself and the opposition. That gives me from 1.3 to 1.5 seconds in which to release the ball. How many steps you take really doesn't make too much difference. You can hop, skip, and jump the rest of the way as long as your first step is about two yards long in the interest of a quick getaway.

Tittle suffered a serious leg injury in the 1963 playoff against the Bears and that is probably what influenced him to retire as a player, because he could still throw the ball at the end of his career.

Legs are generally the first of an athlete's equipment to go. If they are injured and don't heal properly, it's simply too bad. Playing on bad legs means you're just kidding yourself.

A direct opposite to Tittle in style is Fran Tarkenton, who starred for the Minnesota Vikings for the first six years of his career before being traded to the New York Giants. We saw a lot of Franny because we played the Vikings twice each year in the Western Conference, and he always impressed me.

Tarkenton is not a big man. In fact, he's a little smaller than most of us. And he doesn't have an exceptionally strong throwing arm. However, he has something else that maybe one person in ten thousand has. You might call it, "eyes in the back of your head."

This is an ability to sense that people are coming at him from behind. Time and again you'd be watching as someone got ready to take Fran apart from behind or from the blind side. Just when a big 250-pounder would lunge at him, Tarkenton would suddenly dance to one side. The big fellow would go on his face and Fran would keep moving. Lots of us can duck under a tackler, a move which is thrilling enough when seen from the stands but which is fairly routine. Tarkenton's running around back there, however, is a bird of a different hue.

I don't know how they do it with Tarkenton on the Giants, but with Minnesota his receivers were always taught to run the way he was running, and back *toward* him. In other words they actually ran away from the defense.

A lot of Tarkenton's scrambling can be attributed to the fact that the blockers up front have failed. When this happens he must make a hasty attempt to set up a protective pocket in some other section of the field.

Oh, we thought of Tarkenton a lot when he was in our conference. We always tried to have what we called a "controlled rush" on him. We wouldn't come in, hell-bent for election, but we'd try to keep him in the pocket because we found he wasn't as effective in there. As I said, he isn't very tall and if your tackles get a little bit of penetration and keep their arms up, Tarkenton has a problem seeing. But if you come slamming in, and your end gets hooked to the inside, then Tarkenton has a chance to run to the outside. Once he's there he can do pretty much anything he wants to. That's where he's the most effective. After all, he did throw twenty-nine TD passes in his first year with the Giants, which was one-third more than the Giants got the previous season.

Fran lives more dangerously than most of us. He represents a special threat, and his scrambling irritates the big defensive men who think they have him nailed, only to lose him. When they get a shot at him, they usually try to make it a "good one."

Unquestionably, Fran is aware of this. But it hasn't caused him to change his style. And it hasn't prevented him from becoming one of the top-flight box-office attractions of the game.

Quarterbacks can't permit themselves to think of injuries, or they'll leave their game in the locker room. And they have to learn to ignore minor hurts and sometimes even major ones. I've had a broken vertebra, broken ribs, and a punctured lung. In 1963 I played with a swollen middle finger on my throwing hand right from the opening game when I stuck it into some would-be Giant tackler's helmet.

Broken ribs hurt, some more than most. If you get a broken rib at the bottom or at the top chances are it won't bother you too much, although you certainly will know you have it. Break the ones in the middle, though, where you get a lot of movement from breathing, and you'll be a little sore, especially with someone banging on them every once in a while.

Once a game starts a good athlete will tend to forget what's bothering him and concentrate on doing the job, even though the pain is always there. You just lift yourself a notch or two above it. No one teaches you how it's done. Somehow, the good football players know this technique instinctively.

Okay, let's have a look now at some of the games that brought the best players together, sometimes for the championship, sometimes in the regular season. Perhaps there might be an unfamiliar name or two, particularly in the early years. Remember, though, without these men, the pro game might have taken just a little longer to gain acceptance. One game today might attract as many persons as these men played before during an entire season, but they were the best of their time. Chances are they'd have been able to give a pretty good account of themselves at any period in the game's history.

THE GAME: *Chicago vs. New York*
THE PLACE: *New York City*
THE TIME: *December 9, 1934*
FINAL SCORE: *New York, 30; Chicago, 13*

2. Be Careful, It's Slippery

Football games are won by blocking, tackling, passing, and running, with kicking thrown in for good measure. Once in a very great while, a game is won because someone remembers something that happened under similar circumstances—or someone has enough sense to say, "Take a cab, don't fool around with the subway."

That's what decided the 1934 National Football League championship playoff. That's what gave the New York Giants the first of their many titles.

The NFL playoff system was introduced in 1933. The Bears won in the West, the Giants in the East. The Bears took the playoff by a score of 23–21, and each player walked off the field in Chicago with the munificent sum of $210.23.

Now these same two teams were back for the 1934 playoff in New York. College football, which was king in those days, was wrapped up and put away for the year, except for a post-season bowl or two. The pros had the field more or less to themselves. Surprisingly, there was a good deal of acceptance by the press, which previously had largely ignored the play-for-pay brand of the game. This was pretty remarkable considering that less than a decade earlier Tim Mara, of the Giants, had paid five hundred dollars for a New York franchise. When asked why he was throwing away five hundred dollars on a sport that didn't have a chance, Mara got off a line that is still quoted: "A franchise for *anything* in New York is worth five hundred dollars."

Over the years the phrase "Mara luck" has become popular in New York sports circles. It refers to the good fortune the Giants' management has had with the weather for almost a half-century. Of course it hasn't worked out 100 percent, but it always seemed that no matter how bad the weather was the day before, the sun would be shining the day the Giants played at home.

Well, the sun might have been shining for other games, but for the first playoff game at the Polo Grounds the weather was best suited for an Eskimo vacation. The temperature was down around zero; the wind cut like a knife. It had been wet most of the week and the moisture, sitting on top of what had been the playing turf at the ball park, was now a sheet of glass, broken occasionally by patches of non-ice.

It was most fortunate that Jack Mara, president of the club and Tim's older son, had gone over early for a look. He called Steve Owen, who was to coach the Giants for a quarter-century, and advised him that the field would be far better suited for hockey than for football.

Steve was at the hotel where most of the players lived. At breakfast a short time later he communicated the gloomy news to his captain, Ray Flaherty, an all-league end and in later years a head coach himself. Flaherty's reaction was to suggest wearing sneakers. "We ran into this same situation back at Gonzaga," he explained, "and we put on sneakers and we beat Montana silly."

Owen liked the idea, then suddenly didn't like it. "It's

Sunday," he said morosely. "Where are we going to get sneakers?"

No stores were open, of course, and a last hope died when they phoned Ken Strong, who was living in town and working for a sporting goods concern. Strong, a superstar of that era, said he had the keys to the office, but not to the building and that he had tried to get into the building on other Sundays without success.

So off everyone went to the ball park, resigned to do figure-8s for the afternoon. In the dressing room Owen brought up the subject again, this time with his trainers. "Where in hell can we get some sneakers? I'll bet there are a million pairs within ten miles of this park."

His trainers, Gus Mauch and Charley Porter, also worked with Manhattan College's teams. They had come up to that school when John F. (Chick) Meehan had left New York University and moved his brand of football farther uptown. Along with Meehan went a long-time admirer, Abe Cohen, a tailor who had entered sports via the back door of a campus tailor shop. Cohen had accompanied Chick to Manhattan to run his athletic storeroom. Woe unto the kid who tried to swipe as much as a shoelace!

This trio, Mauch, Porter, and Cohen, looked at each other. Said Mauch, "We got all kinds of sneakers up at the college." And reaching into his pocket, "Here are the keys to the lockers. Someone will have to go up there and get them."

Abe Cohen hustled into his coat without a word. As he reached the door, Owen called, "Take a cab, Abe, don't fool with the subway."

The Giants played the first half in regulation cleats. So did the Bears. They skated around desperately clutching for each other. The Giants would fling themselves at Bronko Nagurski, the Bears' great fullback, then slide five or six

yards under Bronko's forward impetus. Strong, the Giants'
ace, had a bad leg, made doubly troublesome by his
inability to maintain normal footing. He kicked a thirty-
eight-yard field goal, and then the Bears picked up a
touchdown and a field goal, missing two other field goals.
Chicago had a 10–3 lead at the half.

Mauch and Porter were busily ministering to the bruised
and aching Giants when the clubhouse door was flung open
to permit a wild-eyed, tousle-haired Abe Cohen to stagger
in with a load of sneakers. He looked like some housewife
who had just had a large bag of groceries burst moments
after she left the supermarket.

But Abe hadn't dropped a single piece of footgear. "Nine
pairs," he gasped. "That's all I was able to get." He got
them by using the master key on the lockers in the gym-
nasium. History doesn't record who the sneakers belonged
to, or what the original owners said about the condition
they found them in when they went to use them again.

Steve's brother Bill, a lineman, tried on a pair that
looked as though they might be his size and went outside to see how they'd handle on ice. A moment later he
was back, smiling. "Great," he announced. "They hold a
lot better than the cleats."

So the backs and the ends rummaged through the pile
for their sizes, and when it came time to return to the
field they were still rummaging. Outside George Halas
wondered aloud what was holding up the Giants. He was
freezing, and he wanted to get the game over with.

Reported a substitute guard, Walt Kiesling, "They're
changing into sneakers."

Halas made a sound that was a cross between a snort
and a laugh. "Sneakers? Great," he said, loud enough for
everyone near him to hear. "Step on their toes."

Ed Danowski, the Giants' quarterback, had decided

against putting on the sneakers. But the first two times he carried the ball he slipped for losses. He called time out and skidded across to the bench. "See whether you got a pair of 12s, Gus," he called.

In the third quarter the Bears got another field goal, stretching their lead to 13–3, and it looked as though the crowd would get early relief from the cold. However, as the third quarter ended the Giants, getting the feel of the new footgear, began to move. Once they did they never stopped. The New Yorkers scored twenty-seven points in that final fifteen minutes, still a playoff record.

Ike Frankian ripped an interception from Carl Brumbaugh's hands for a TD, Strong ran forty-two yards for another, and followed it with the Giants' only reverse of the game for a third.

The Bears were now rattled, and after an interception, Danowski cut outside his right end for a final touchdown. After it was all over the Bears remarked bitterly that the sneakers had been the edge. Said Nagurski: "They could cut, and we couldn't."

The winners' shares were $621, almost three times that of the previous year. With one or two exceptions in the late 1930s and early 1940s, the playoff share has never gone any way but up.

It was single-platoon football in those days, and the Giants had made only four substitutions, five if you count Johnny Dell Isola, who sent himself in for Mel Hein, the center, during an interlude when the crowd had to be cleared from the field. A tough and spirited performer, Dell Isola simply couldn't keep out of the action.

Abe Cohen spent the rest of his days working with college teams at Manhattan. He was one person who never needed a ticket to see the Giants in the days when packed houses became commonplace. His hustle had brought

New York its first playoff crown, and the management never forgot it.

If the taxi driver who drove Abe that day had showed up he'd probably have gotten in for nothing, too.

THE GAME: *New York vs. Detroit*
THE PLACE: *Detroit*
THE TIME: *December 19, 1935*
FINAL SCORE: *Detroit, 26; New York, 7*

3. The Lions' First Title

The Lions were the third team to win a playoff title. They did it in their native Detroit, where they had moved a couple of seasons earlier from Portsmouth, Ohio. In moving they had changed their nickname from "Spartans." "Lions" seemed to go well with "Tigers," the popular baseball club in town.

The Lions beat the Giants in the rain, mud, slush, and snow of the University of Detroit's stadium. Everything about that day is "estimated," including the depth of the snowdrifts on the field when the game ended. There were supposed to be fifteen thousand in the stands and the winners are supposed to have received three hundred dollars, the losers one hundred dollars less. Today, every pro game, even preseason contests, is carefully documented down to the final couple of inches. The 1935 playoff was so casual an affair that there is no actual play-by-play record available. The National Football League has a standing offer of a season pass to anyone who produces a valid one.

There is probably an excellent reason for the lack of records on this championship game. The stadium was completely uncovered. Everyone was at the mercy of the elements, which had been playing volleyball with the Mid-west for a full week. Any kind of writing paper exposed for a couple of minutes quickly became a soggy mess.

Detroit was one of the more unusual clubs to win a championship. In 1933 the Lions had been runners-up to the Bears in the West, giving Motor City fans hopes that a first-class pro football operation had finally come to town after a lot of shoestring, quick-buck disappointments. Then they slipped in 1934, the year the Tigers won the baseball pennant, and fans cooled quickly. With a 3-3-2 record past the halfway mark the Lions didn't seem to have much of a chance.

But the Lions, coached by George (Potsy) Clark, and directed on the field by Earl (Dutch) Clark, a Hall of Fame quarterback, caught fire coming down the stretch and won four in a row. They actually won fewer games (seven) than did Green Bay (eight), but the ties, nor-mally something you'd think of as a millstone, actually helped.

The NFL had then, and still has, a system of discarding ties and figuring the remaining won-lost for the percentage that determines where a team finishes. The Lions' 7-3-2 was good for .700, Green Bay's 8-4 for .666, and suddenly the Giants, who had played everyone in the league except the Lions that year, found themselves on the New York Central's *Wolverine,* bumping their way to Detroit.

The Giants had bumped the Eastern Division around pretty thoroughly, winning four more games than their closest rivals. They might have taken the Detroit game a little too nonchalantly.

Potsy Clark shepherded his men into secret drills, and from these he issued statements which indicated that it would be nice if something happened to hamper the Giants' passing combination of Ed Danowski to Tod Goodwin, the rookie who led the league's receivers. Off what happened he could have hired himself out as a rain-maker, because for twenty-four hours there was steady pre-cipitation, and not of the merely dripping variety, either. It poured up to game time. Then after a few minutes' lull it began to snow, and it kept at it long after the game had ended.

The customers who showed up risked pre-penicillin pneumonia, which was no joke, but they got the show they came for, a sound trouncing of the haughty Giants by the underrated Lions. The weather made passing dan-gerous, and when forced to rely on a running game the New Yorkers were no match for the Lions, who out-gained them at a 2½–1 ratio. Runners like Ace Gutowski, Clark, Ernie Caddel, and Buddy Parker, who was to coach the Lions in the fifties, all slammed their way to TDs.

Gutowski, who had played briefly with the Giants several years earlier, opened the scoring and Parker closed it. One of Danowski's four completions was a twenty-five-yarder to Ken Strong on the Detroit thirty, and the Giant star went scooting down the sidelines for his team's only score.

Strong also accounted for the extra point. He thus scored in three successive playoffs, which is quite some-thing, when you consider what the odds were, and are, on a team making the playoff three years in a row.

The Lions, that year, were the third-best rushing club in NFL history, piling up 2763 yards. They celebrated the rushing mark, their victory over the Giants, and other ac-complishments of the season by embarking on a twelve-thousand-mile-long playing junket to such spots as South-ern California and Honolulu. They had won their title in the snow but had seen enough of the stuff for one year.

THE GAME: *New York vs. Washington*
THE PLACE: *Washington, D.C.*
THE TIME: *September 20, 1942*
FINAL SCORE: *New York, 14; Washington, 7*

4. A Slight Case of Mirrors

Sharpened by proximity and the publicity that stemmed from ten daily newspapers in New York and half that number in Washington, the football rivalry between the New York Giants and the Washington Redskins was, for years, the keenest in the National League. For Giant games in Griffith Stadium, the Washington impresario, George P. Marshall, used to put in an early call for extra police to help turn away the extra customers. For the games in New York he led as many as ten thousand frenzied adherents through eight hours' worth of round-trip train ride to and from the Big Town, and threw in a parade up Broadway, with brass band and high-stepping "Indian" maidens, none of whom had ever seen a reservation.

There were occasional setbacks for Washington. The Bears' 73–0 playoff victory in 1940 still stands as the most lopsided score in the history of the league's title game. But Redskin rooters recovered rapidly. In 1942 they figured they had the big team in the league despite their third-place finish behind the Giants in the Eastern Division the year before, a record which included two defeats by New York.

For one thing, the Giants had been hit hard by the

war's drain. Nello Falaschi, their championship club quarterback, was gone, and rookies had filled in at a good many spots.

The levy on the Redskins hadn't been quite as severe. They still had the incomparable Sammy Baugh calling the shots and staging his one-man aerial circus.

The first of the home-and-home series with New York was set for Griffith Stadium, and the Redskins warmed up with a two-touchdown victory over the Steelers. For the New York game 34,700 fans, most of them in shirt-sleeves, were jammed into the park. It was a fine, late September Sunday afternoon. The band blared, the spurious redfaces scalped cringing palefaces, and the customers howled for the Giants' front teeth.

Other locations might boast a heavier annual rainfall, but the nation's capital yields to none in the dubious distinction of having a quick-gathering storm rush in from the Blue Ridge foothills. Fifteen minutes before the kickoff it was a beautiful afternoon; by the time the Redskins got possession, the park was an aquarama.

Jim Lee Howell, Giant end and later New York's head coach and director of personnel, recalled that an errant ball actually floated, rather than rolled, away. And in that brief span the Redskins' undefeated season floated from their grasp.

The Giants had returned the opening kickoff to midfield, and on the first play they shifted into left formation, with Tuffy Leemans, the hard-driving fullback, receiving the snap from center. Leemans faked to the reversing Ward Cuff, then threw a long pass into the left-half zone. Will Walls timed it for a perfect over-the-shoulder catch. He scampered twenty-five yards for the touchdown and the Redskins were undone.

Then the storm hit. In two minutes the customers were

wetter than the players, and it was a little difficult to tell them apart. The field turned into a swamp, and the desperate Redskins cast about for a means of catching up.

They were clearly the superior team. Despite the horrendous conditions they could still move the ball, thanks to Baugh's passing (twelve of nineteen) and his field generalship. Their defense was also excellent; the Giants couldn't budge the ball.

In the second period Washington tied it with a forty-five-yard scoring march, topped by a plunge by Bob Seymour. In the third they were en route to another when the roof fell in. Dick Poillon, Baugh's rookie replacement, whipped a flanker pass to Andy Farkas, who forgot to look. O'Neale Adams, a Giant end, snatched the ball and ran sixty-six yards for the second touchdown. Farkas was in position to bring down the interceptor had he turned. He never did.

That wrapped it up, and the Giants were still on top when the game ended. The final figures were incredible. The Redskins had fifteen first downs to the Giants' none. They outrushed the Giants 232 yards to one.

Except for the intercepted pass the Giants had never trespassed beyond the Redskins' thirty-eight-yard line at any time after their first touchdown.

The following day dawned sunny, clear, and windless. Washington would gladly have replayed the game on a night's sleep. "We'll kill 'em when we get up to the Polo Grounds," vowed the angry Redskins.

They didn't, although they did win, oddly by the same 14–7 score. Then Washington went on to take the world championship from the Chicago Bears, a title which had to satisfy them for the next quarter-century.

THE GAME: *Cleveland vs. Philadelphia*
THE PLACE: *Philadelphia*
THE TIME: *September 16, 1950*
FINAL SCORE: *Cleveland, 35; Philadelphia, 10*

5. Clash of the Juggernauts

During his ten years of professional football, Otto Graham won a great many important games for the Cleveland Browns in both the All-America Conference and the National League. In the former he led them to four successive championships. After the leagues merged, he was at the helm of a half-dozen conference championship clubs as well as three playoff winners.

It is doubtful, however, whether any single victory in which Graham participated had the impact of the opening game of the 1950 season, the year that peace came to pro football for a decade after a bitter struggle at the TV-less gate, which neither league could win.

The Cleveland Browns had dominated the short-lived Conference, originally the brainchild of Chicago *Tribune* sports editor Arch Ward, not because there was a lack of talent, but because they were a superb club. Graham led the league in passing every year. His receivers, Mac Speedie and Dante Lavelli, came to be bywords of excellence, and Marion Motley was the outstanding power runner the new loop produced. It was generally acknowledged that Paul Brown, after whom the team was named, was several years ahead of his contemporaries in both coaching and methodology. If Brown never contributed anything else to pro ball, and he contributed many, many things, the carefully documented "itineraries" for a football trip, on which practically every moment of a player's time is accounted for, from breakfast to bedtime, could be his memorial. In the late forties the Browns' "travel orders" told the ballplayers how many pats of butter to put on a pregame baked potato at a time when most clubs didn't know where their players were eating, and didn't much care.

Neither Brown nor his ball club was held in particularly high regard in the National League. Most NFL clubs didn't even bother to scout the Conference, figuring it wasn't going to last too long, anyway. The AAC commissioners, who changed practically every season, would respond annually with a challenge for a world championship.

They got it, but only after the "merger" which wiped out every ACC team except the Browns, the 49ers, and the Baltimore Colts (which died the following year, and was revived a few years later).

Bert Bell, commissioner of the NFL, was years ahead of his time as a sports executive. Bell knew a good promotional situation when he saw one. His Eagles ("his" because at one time he had owned the Philadelphia club, and although he came from a Main Line family he wasn't too proud to help peddle tickets on a Saturday afternoon) had blanked the Rams in the NFL playoff the previous year. They were the idols of the Quaker City. Why not bring them together with the Browns as quickly as possible? And what could be better than to open the season with a matchup in Philadelphia?

Bell figured it would fill Municipal Stadium, the great big white elephant that has slumbered on the South Side of Philadelphia for more than forty years, quietly awaiting its once-a-year hundred-thousand crowd for the Army-Navy game.

Well, it didn't quite fill the stadium, but 71,237 customers backed up Bell's evaluation of the game's possibilities as a late-summer draw. It was played on a Saturday night in mid-September, and it attracted more customers than any previous professional game in Philadelphia's history.

The Browns drew scant respect from Philadelphia's players, who reflected the attitude of their hard-bitten coach, Earl (Greasy) Neale. "The Browns?" he scoffed. "They're nothing more than a lot of basketball players."

Neale, of course, had Steve Van Buren, a runner who had set a NFL record of 1146 yards the previous year and whose 196 yards against the Rams the previous December still stands as a championship playoff record.

But what the Eagles didn't realize was that the Browns' balanced attack could put enormous pressure on even the best of clubs. They paid for their nonchalance with a 35–10 beating.

The Eagles scored first on a fifteen-yard field goal by Cliff Patton, but only because a punt return by Cleveland's Don Phelps for eighty yards and a touchdown was nullified by a clipping penalty.

After that the Browns poured it on. Graham hit with three touchdown passes, one each to Dub Jones, Dante Lavelli, and Mac Speedie. He also scored on a sneak in the second half. Rex Baumgardner chipped in with a touchdown late in the game on a short run. Motley's main contribution was a ferocious piece of defensive play when the Eagles got to the two-yard line on a first down and failed to punch it across.

Graham completed twenty-one of thirty-eight passes that night for 346 yards. He had thrown eighty-six TD passes in his four years in the Conference (they played a fourteen-game schedule), and he passed for eighty-eight more in his six years in the NFL. He did a lot more running in the NFL, tripling his yardage and his scoring in this category.

When he retired after the 1956 season the Browns won only one more conference crown, then didn't win again for a half-dozen seasons.

6. The Incredible Spec Sanders

No look at the long-departed All-America Conference can begin to be complete without a reference to Orban (Spec) Sanders, who set all kinds of records in one brilliant campaign in 1947. Sanders was an Oklahoman who came out of the Navy to star with the New York Yankees. He performed out of the single wing, played two ways as did everyone else, and had a short fling at defense after the leagues merged.

He was such an outstanding player that after he made the switch to defensive back, because of a knee injury, he was able to equal the then-current record of thirteen interceptions. It makes you wonder what he would have done as a one-way offensive performer in today's game.

In the single wing, the best ballplayer usually played in the tailback spot. He ran with the ball, threw most of the passes, and kicked. These were Spec's assignments. In 1947 he carried the ball 231 times for a total of 1432 yards and eighteen TDs. These marks were to stand for a dozen years. Jim Brown broke the yardage mark, Jim Taylor, the touchdowns.

During the same season he also threw fourteen TD passes, returned a kickoff for a touchdown, and made three

interceptions. He scored 114 points. Sanders' biggest individual effort came in the first part of the season when
he registered 250 yards against the Chicago Rockets in
Soldier Field. It was a Friday night game and it barely
got a mention. Today it would have provided national
headlines. No one came close to that figure until Cookie
Gilchrist rushed 243 yards for Buffalo against New York
in 1963.

What helped make Sanders effective that big year was
the emergence of Buddy Young. Buddy was a speed demon
who barely measured five-six and weighed only 160 pounds.
Every time he handled the ball he was a threat to go all
the way, so the opposition couldn't key exclusively on
Spec. Buddy survived the merger of the leagues and made
it to a couple of clubs before winding up with the Colts.
He was just finishing up in 1956 when I arrived.

Sanders played for Texas and had been overshadowed
by a lot of All-Americans. He played service ball with
Pre-Flight teams at Georgia and North Carolina, and when
he came out of the service he was ready. Technically he
was under contract to the Redskins because he had signed
with them in his last year in college. But when Ray
Flaherty, the Redskins coach, switched to the rival league,
Spec went along with him.

Young recalls Sanders' style and his ability to absorb
punishment. "Tough as nails," says Buddy. "After every
game he was a mass of bruises from his hips down."

"What fooled them," Young remembers, "was his gait.
It was longer than it looked. If you had measured it you'd
probably find it was as long as Gale Sayers' today. He
had a kind of glide, the same as Sayers. I've always considered him part of a select group of runners like Hugh
McElhenny, George Taliaferro, Marion Motley, Jim Brown,
Lenny Moore, and Sayers."

The All-America Conference made certain definite con-
tributions to the pro game. It demonstrated the attractive-
ness of a fourteen-game schedule, for one thing. That's
the format of the game for the foreseeable future. It demonstrated, too, that dependence solely upon the gate was too
risky a proposition so that when coast-to-coast TV came
along the owners were able to make financial use of it.

Sanders played only for the benefit of those who came
through the turnstiles and for local TV audiences. Today
he'd have been a national sports figure. In the musty
record books his 250 yards rushing in a single game shines
with the brilliance of a neon sign.

THE GAME: *Los Angeles vs. Cleveland*
THE PLACE: *Los Angeles*
THE TIME: *December 23, 1951*
FINAL SCORE: *Los Angeles, 21; Cleveland, 17*

7. *The Tube Goes Coast to Coast*

The first championship football playoff to be telecast nationally was that between the Rams and the Browns from the Coliseum in Los Angeles. The technical brain behind it, Allan B. Dumont, who owned his own network, is gone. So is the fellow who handled the play-by-play, Harry Wismer.

Harry had a modest amount of collegiate experience as a reserve quarterback at Michigan, and was later an owner in the American League. He was known for injecting an extra bit of color into the proceedings, like waving a friendly "hello" to people who were a good thousand miles from the ball park in which Harry said they were. Sometimes they had difficulty explaining where they actually were. And Wismer didn't care whether you were a U.S. postman or a U.S. senator. He once "waved hello" to Damon Runyon, the famed columnist, who had been dead for ten years.

Wismer was partial to colorful adjectives, but for this first transcontinental TV effort he didn't have to use many. The drama was all there, thanks to one of the greatest offensive units in the history of the Rams, and one of the most memorable passes in the history of the game.

Before 1951, TV sports programing was a haphazard affair. It seems incredible that the big revenue for clubs then selling broadcast rights came from radio, not TV. TV cameras were customarily pushed into some dusty corner.

The exciting baseball race in the National League that year changed things, and it's never been the same since. Today TV is sufficiently important so that a man like George Halas of the Bears, one of pro football's founding fathers, has stated flatly that the game couldn't exist in its present form without the revenue from TV.

The 1951 pennant race between the Brooklyn Dodgers and the New York Giants ended in a tie on the final day of the season, necessitating a three-game playoff. Walter F. O'Malley, boss of the Dodgers, stayed up that night selling the TV rights to the Columbia Broadcasting System. The network took a gamble on the tremendous interest which had been generated. Bear in mind that major-league baseball, unlike major-league football, hadn't made its way out to the West Coast yet.

Up to that point TV itself was a patchy arrangement, with hookups extending from New York to Washington, from Los Angeles to San Francisco, from Chicago to Cleveland, etc., with large gaps in between. The Dodgers and Giants put them all together for the first time, making it feasible for football to go national the following December.

There was plenty of interest in a Rams-Browns championship playoff. They had met twice before, in the 1950 title game which Cleveland had won 30–28, and during the 1951 season, when the Browns had won again, 38–23. Moreover, the Rams were originally from Cleveland, having moved a half-dozen years previously when they won the championship, yet finished in the red.

The Rams didn't prosper their first few years in Los

Angeles, either, involved as they were in a life-and-death
struggle with the Los Angeles Dons of the rival All-
America Conference. Both shared the Coliseum, and the
Dons (named after screen star Don Ameche, who was one
of the owners) were a better draw until the Conference
collapsed after the 1949 season and was absorbed into the
NFL.

In 1950 the Rams negotiated a historic TV deal, which
has never been tried since. Dan Reeves, the Rams' owner,
figured out what the break-even attendance per game
would be, and got a sponsor to agree to pay the difference
in cash between that figure and what actually came in
at the gate. At season's end the sponsor turned over a
check for more than three hundred thousand dollars, prov-
ing definitely that you can't sell your product and give it
away at the same time. But what this experiment had done
was to create a lot of new fans. When the word got out
that it wouldn't be free any more, the people who had
been hooked by pro football on TV the previous year
turned out at the ball park.

The Rams were in the playoff for a third straight year.
In 1949 they had been shut out by the Philadelphia Eagles,
whose great runner, Steve Van Buren, set a playoff rushing
record of 196 yards. The following year they had been
beaten by Lou Groza's last-minute field goal. Now they
had another shot and they had a team that was loaded
with talent.

The quarterbacks, Bob Waterfield and Norm Van Brocklin, were both to go on to major coaching jobs, as was
their record receiver, Tom Fears. Joe Stydahar, the former
Bear who coached the Rams, didn't quite know how to
handle all the quarterbacking talent he had available. His
problem was, he didn't know who to start. So he alternated
starters and then alternated the two men each period.

Other teams have done this since, but never with players like Van Brocklin and Waterfield.

Cleveland had a 10–7 lead at the half, although the Rams had scored first on a fifty-five-yard drive climaxed by Dick Hoerner's one-yard plunge. Cleveland came back with a record field goal by Groza which traveled fifty-two yards. Then Otto Graham connected with three passes, the last to Dub Jones for seventeen yards and a touchdown.

Shortly after play was resumed the Rams got a break. Graham was rushed and fumbled the ball. Andy Robustelli, a rookie lineman, grabbed the ball but had difficulty holding it because his hands had been tightly wrapped with tape before the game started. He managed to balance the ball gingerly on his fingertips while he sped as far as the Cleveland one, where he was brought down. Dan Towler then scored for Los Angeles.

A Waterfield field goal (he was the league's second-best scorer that year in addition to being the leading passer), put the Rams ahead, but the Browns went seventy yards in ten plays, including a thirty-four-yard carry down the sideline by Graham. Again it was tied up.

Now Van Brocklin was directing the Rams. From his own twenty he dropped back to the fourteen, looking for Tom Fears. Fears was running a long down-and-in pattern. Van Brocklin's pass reached him just as he passed between Tom James and Cliff Lewis. He wheeled and sped toward the line, sixty yards away.

Fears had set a record of eighty-four receptions the previous year, but had been replaced as the Ram's primary target by Elroy Hirsch, who had been converted from running back to end in 1951. Few could match Fears' receiving ability, but there were any number of players who could match his speed. Players, for instance, like the two Cleveland defenders he had temporarily outwitted.

As they took after him every spectator felt they'd over-haul Fears in a few steps. But from somewhere Fears managed to generate speed which neither he or anyone else knew he had. They gained on him in that mad dash toward the Cleveland goal line, but they did it only inch by inch. And those original couple of steps' advantage he had when he caught the ball proved sufficient. With seven minutes left, Fears crossed the line untouched, scoring the winning touchdown.

It was to be ten years before the National League, early in Pete Rozelle's tenure as commissioner, agreed to put all its TV into one package, a move which brought undreamed-of prosperity. But pro football on TV first had to have a start that made it both attractive and competitive in an era of Howdy Doody, Milton Berle, and Ed Wynn. The Van Brocklin-to-Fears winning pass was about as good an introduction as any.

8. Layne in the Clutch

Bobby Layne was one of the more colorful quarterbacks in the history of the pros, and it wasn't simply because everyone except Bobby had placed wisdom above valor and had gone for the face masks by the mid-1950s. Bobby, who played fourteen years in the big leagues, never bothered with a bar of any kind, seeming to invite an occasional poke in the jaw. He had a sharp tongue that went along with an even sharper football brain. There was more than one member of the opposition who was eventually goaded into taking an exasperated swing.

Bobby took the Detroit Lions to four conference titles and three world championships in their golden years, the first half of the 1950s. In 1951 he passed for twenty-six touchdowns, and at that time there were only two players who had hit with more: Sid Luckman of the 1943 Bears with twenty-eight, and Frankie Albert of the 1948 San Francisco 49ers with twenty-nine (in a fourteen-game schedule). Layne's best years came when we were playing twelve-game schedules.

To my mind the 1957 Lions were one of the great teams I've seen or played against. They started with an almost insurmountable handicap, loss of their championship coach

two days before the pre-season schedule started. At a wel-
come-Lions party, Buddy Parker, head man in the 1952,
1953, and 1954 championship drives, the first two of which
had culminated in the playoff title, was called on to say
a few words. He certainly did.

As the diners leaned back to enjoy some of Buddy's
wry humor, he hit 'em fast. "I'm quitting," he announced.
"I can no longer control this team and when I can't
control it I can't coach it."

That ended the party. The startled management hastily
pressed George Wilson, onetime Bears' lineman, into the
breach and Wilson wound up a world championship coach
that year, which merely proves that you never know what's
going to happen when you get up in the morning.

The story is that Layne learned of Parker's sudden re-
solve a short time before Buddy made his epochal an-
nouncement. They had gone into the men's room to spruce
up. "What are you going to say that you haven't already
said, coach?" asked Layne, half-joking.

"I'm going to tell them that I'm quitting. That's what."

Layne never blinked an eye. "Fine," he said, "I'll go
with you."

"You shut up and stay here," snapped Parker. Layne
did, and played on his last championship club. The next
year Parker, who had moved over to the Pittsburgh Steelers, traded for him. Layne finished up on clubs that
struggled to top the .500 mark.

To win the championship in 1957 everyone agreed that
the Lions would have to climb over us. We had won only
five of twelve games in my first year with the Colts, but
we had a fine young team that had only one way to go.
We got off to a fast start by winning our first three games,
including one over the Bears, who had been crushed in

the 1956 playoff by the Giants and whose fire was to take some time to rekindle.

Detroit had dropped its 1957 opener (to us, and by twenty points), so we were reasonably confident that we could do it again out there in Briggs Stadium in the fourth game of the year.

It looked like another easy ride because we had a 27–10 lead after three periods and big Tobin Rote wasn't moving them very much.

They missed with a field-goal attempt by Jim Martin from the forty-two, and in the next series Darris McCord and one or two others got through. They dumped me for a nineteen-yard loss on our ten. We punted to give them the ball at midfield, and Wilson switched to Bobby Layne.

Layne completed three passes in succession, the last of which carried twenty-six yards for a touchdown to Howard Cassady. There were eight minutes left and we still had a ten-point lead after Layne converted, so we still weren't terribly worried.

The next scene was a wild one. We picked up a first down on our thirty-nine. Then on third down of the next series I hit Jim Mutscheller with a pass on the Detroit forty-two. Mutscheller fumbled and Carl Karilivacz, a Detroit defensive back, picked it up and ran sixteen yards to our forty-two where *he* fumbled. There was a big pileup and the officials ruled that Johnny Call, one of our backs, had recovered. This steamed up the Detroit coaching staff so much that they drew a penalty, which put us on the Detroit forty-three.

We stayed on the ground for two plays, then I tried a pass to Call and Karilivacz picked it off on the Lion thirty-two. He returned it three yards. They called us for fouling on the play and that gave the Lions possession at midfield.

Now it looked like our turn. Layne tried a pass to Dorne

Dibble, but Andy Nelson intercepted it on our thirty-eight and took it back to midfield. Meanwhile that clock kept moving right along.

But the "turnovers" hadn't finished. On the second running play Alan Ameche hit right tackle. He fumbled, and Jim David picked it up and got six yards before he was stopped on our forty-six.

Layne missed with a couple of passes, then hit Cassady for eight yards. There were two minutes left and they needed two touchdowns to beat us. We remained reasonably confident.

John Henry Johnson, who was playing his first year with the Lions, went around left end for seven yards and a first down on the thirty-one. Layne then threaded the needle for a thirty-yarder in the corner and a first down on our one-yard line. When Johnson took it over left tackle, there was still a minute and a half to go.

After the kickoff we tried three running plays from deep in our territory. No sense putting the ball up in the air where there was a chance of an interception. On the third play Lenny Moore tried to go around left end and fumbled. Yale Lary recovered on our twenty-nine.

Layne didn't waste any time. Cassady had been his best target, and Cassady was waiting for a pass in the end zone, a completion which almost tore apart the ball park.

When we got the ball for a final try there were thirty-four seconds left. We worked an Ameche-to-Call lateral for five yards, but the show ended on the next play when I fumbled. The Lions grabbed the ball for one running play before the gun.

I remember one odd thing about that game. It must have taken a lot out of both clubs because we both lost our next two. Green Bay beat us for one of their three

victories that year. So did Pittsburgh. Detroit lost to Los
Angeles and San Francisco in successive weeks on the
West Coast. The Lions recovered, however, to beat San
Francisco in a playoff after each had finished with 8–4
records, and then went on to crush Cleveland in the
championship game, 59–14.

The following year we whacked them twice pretty thoroughly en route to our first championship, but that last
period against the 1957 Lions, with Layne driving them
hard, is a memory that'll stick with me forever.

Bobby used to say, half-kiddingly, "I've never lost a
game but sometimes time has run out on me." He had
enough left that afternoon back in 1957.

THE GAME: *Baltimore vs. New York*
THE PLACE: *New York City*
THE TIME: *December 28, 1958*
FINAL SCORE: *Baltimore, 23; New York, 17*

9. Straight up the Middle

It's been ten years since the first overtime game in the history of the National Football League was played. Fans still tell me it's something they'll never forget. Neither will I, or any of the Colts and Giants who were in it. It was the first time the Colts were to emerge as champions of the entire pro football world, quite a development when you consider that only a half-dozen years earlier the club had been a doormat. (The seventy points scored by the Los Angeles Rams against the 1950 Colts had stood as a regular-season record until Washington registered seventy-two against the 1966 Giants.)

The 1958 Colts were a first-rate club. It wasn't any fluke that we were in the championship game, and the same goes for the Giants. We were a young club and had been lucky with injuries, always a factor in any football season. A good many of our players hit their peaks that year, peaks which they maintained through the following year to give Baltimore successive world championships.

One of our top stars was Alan (The Horse) Ameche, who was our heavy-duty runner. Alan was out of Wisconsin, and his nickname traced to his iron-like durability. He was a substantial 225, and from the knees up you

1. This is one of me in my working clothes—with the exception of the hat, which all well-dressed football players must wear. *(Courtesy of the Baltimore Colts)*

2. My favorite receiver, Raymond Berry, making one of his more spectacular catches. *(Photo by Dick Gibson)*

3. Sometimes the receivers are covered. Then a quarterback has to decide he'd better get going. *(Photo by Herb Carleton)*

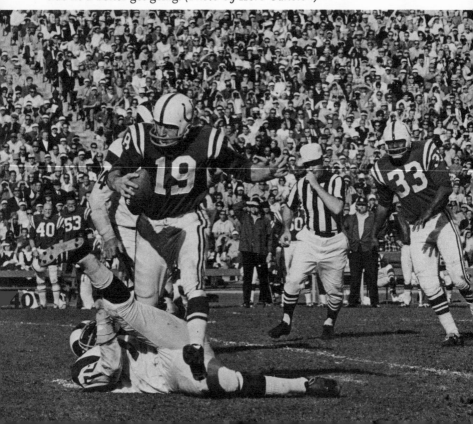

4. Ken Strong's talented toe helps the Giants score a victory in the 1934 NFL title playoff against the Bears in New York's Polo Grounds. *(UPI)*

5. The New York Yankees' triple-threat, Orban (Spec) Sanders, moving around end against the Cleveland Browns in one of the spectacular New York-Cleveland games which were highlights of the short-lived All-America Conference. *(UPI)*

6. Despite a formidable obstacle, Detroit quarterback Bobby Layne gets off a pass against the Rams in the 1957 championship game. *(UPI)*

7. This is the play that decided the first overtime championship game in 1958: Alan Ameche's slam up the middle. That's me on the right leaving the arena for a hot shower. *(UPI)*

8. This run was good for fifteen yards in the 1959 game against the Giants in Baltimore. L. G. DuPre is out in front. *(UPI)*

9. Frank Gifford lies unconscious on Yankee Stadium's turf after a smashing tackle by the Eagles' Chuck Bednarik. The Eagles were champs that year, beating Green Bay in the playoff. *(Wide World)*

10. Billy Cannon, of the Oilers, scores the only touchdown in the 1961 AFL championship game in beating San Diego, 10–3. *(UPI)*

11. Green Bay's great fullback, Jim Taylor, smashes into the line in the 1962 title game. The Packers beat the Giants, 16-7, on that bitter, sub-freezing afternoon. *(Wide World)*

12. **Was the great Jim Brown stopped short of the goal line on this one? If he was, it was one of the rare occasions that the game's most gifted runner had been handled in this fashion.** *(Photo by Tony Tomsic)*

13. Jimmy Brown could also follow his interference, as shown here. *(Photo by Tony Tomsic)*

couldn't have ordered a man better built for the job. He had heavy thighs and a deep chest. It usually required more than one tackler to bring him down. He was good for close to eight hundred yards that year and was a perfect complement to Lenny Moore, a swifty from Penn State who was to last a half-dozen years longer than Alan and was to wind up with a single-season record of twenty touchdowns in 1964.

They had been playing a title game in the NFL since 1933. It seems almost incredible that in a quarter of a century no game would end in a tie, but that's the way it had been. The thought that a tie would eventually pop up had occurred to the owners, however, and a few years before our game the overtime sudden-death rule had been introduced. It was a flip of the coin, the winner having the choice of kicking off or receiving.

Well, we lost the toss that afternoon, but we won the game, and we won it in a way that caused a lot of conversation that winter.

It was a strange game, that '58 playoff. They held us when we got down around the three-yard line after it looked as though we would have no trouble building up a comfortable margin. The ground was frozen there, although the rest of the field was soft, and our runners were amazed to find they couldn't get any kind of footing.

Then the Giants got out in front. We had to catch them in the final two minutes with a field goal by Steve Myhra (in the last seven seconds) after Berry had accounted for seventy-three yards with three fine catches.

There were so many big plays in the game—regular and overtime—that it's a little difficult to single out the outstanding one. There were thirteen plays in the series that won us the title after the regulation game had ended in a 17–17 tie. Let's focus on Ameche's trap up the middle that was good for twenty-three yards. It put us into excellent field position and set things up for the TD five plays later.

We had come from our own twenty after the Giants had been forced to punt. During this series there had been a couple of 12–13 yard passes to Berry, who has caught more passes than any man in football.

Berry was a perfectly marvelous receiver when he was at the top of his abilities. I've seen him lean so far back that he was perfectly parallel to the ground, leaving his feet at the final split second necessary to catch the ball. He was a merciless technician when he was having a good day, and as the shadows in Yankee Stadium lengthened, the Giants' respect for him had steadily increased.

In football, as in everything else, each move has its cause and effect. You move over a little to protect against something that has been damaging you all day and you expose a weakness somewhere else.

There was no question that Berry's receiving was having a powerful influence on the Giants' defensive strategy. To "take the middle away" from Raymond, making it difficult for him to slant in and catch a pass a dozen yards ahead of where our center had originally been stationed, Harland Svare, one of the Giants' outside linebackers, had moved in a bit. Sam Huff, the colorful middle linebacker who starred with both the Giants and the Washington Redskins before his retirement after 1967, had dropped back a bit, with the same defensive tactic in mind.

Ameche was our flare control (some clubs call it the "safety valve,") meaning a running back who becomes available for a pass when the regular receivers are covered. There they were offering an almost airtight defense against a medium-range pass across the middle to Raymond.

So I flipped a short one, perhaps three yards, to Alan, and it was good for seven yards, and a big first down.

On the next play I sent L. G. Dupre, who had been running well for us all afternoon, around our right end. He had a lot of help from Jim Mutscheller, our tight end, who had been doing a fine blocking job on Jim Katcavage, the opposing defensive end, even though Kat had thirty pounds on him.

That was another seven yards and it made it second and three. A pass was called for here, and while I was back looking for either Berry or Mutscheller the Giants really blew in on me and nailed me for a twelve-yard loss. Dick Modzelewski was all over me. He had me before I could even get my arm up to throw.

On the next play I hit Berry with a first-down pass on the Giants' forty-two-yard line. Just prior to the play I noticed that Sam Huff had dropped back in an effort to help out against the short pass. He was four or five yards out of position. Ordinarily he'd be up there pretty tight, maybe three yards from the line of scrimmage.

I had a pass called for the next play. It was to be either Berry or Mutscheller to the inside again. When I saw Huff out of position I did a little fast thinking. Modzelewski would be charging in there real fast hoping to get me again. He should be fairly easily to trap. Huff, deeper than usual, should be an easy block for our strong-side tackle. If he is up there tight the tackle ordinarily can't get to him.

So I switched to a trap play at the line of scrimmage, and everything worked perfectly. Sam hung back and Moe came in like a bull. Art Spinney, the guard, trapped him beautifully, and our center, Buzz Nutter, blocked Spinney's man, Rosey Grier. George Preas, the tackle, went through and blocked Huff, and Ameche had clear sailing for twenty-three yards.

We got to the thirteen with a first down, and a few minutes later we had stowed away the first overtime victory in history. There was one play in this series where some questioned the wisdom of my putting the ball in the air (to Mutscheller in the flat), but there was never any danger because both their outside linebacker and their safety were playing on Jimmy's inside, giving him everything in the flat. On a pass like this, if the halfback leaves his flanker-covering assignment and gets into the play, you can always flip the ball over your tight end's head to put it safely out of bounds. And you don't have to have any exceptional pass-blocking to get off this kind of a pass—three-tenths of a second is all you need because your linemen are firing out aggressively and can hold the rushers for that length of time.

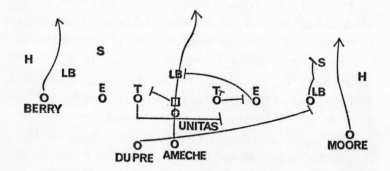

1. Ameche Trap Play

To clear out the middle, the center blocks the right tackle. The right guard brush blocks the opposing left tackle, letting him through to be picked up by the *left* guard, then goes on to block the end. The right tackle picks up the middle linebacker in time to permit Ameche to get through.

THE GAME: *Baltimore vs. New York*
THE PLACE: *Baltimore*
THE TIME: *December 27, 1959*
FINAL SCORE: *Baltimore, 31; New York, 16*

10. Second Time Around

Some of my newspaper friends used to kid about a colleague who was given to making obvious statements. One of their favorites was, "Ten years is a long time, and twenty years is a long, long time."

Perhaps in the same category is "It's pretty tough to lose a ball game if you score a couple of dozen points in the last quarter." The record for a playoff is the twenty-seven racked up by the sneakered New York Giants more than three-score years ago. When we got our two dozen the Giants were the victims. Unlike the sneaker game, or for that matter, the extra-period game of the previous year, this one was played in almost-perfect weather in Baltimore's Memorial Stadium. Anything heavier than a topcoat would have been too warm. We were lucky to get a day like that around Christmastime.

We were lucky, too, to stop the Giants' determined bid in the late moments of the third period when they were in front 9–7, thanks to three successful field goals by the talented Pat Summerall. They went for six points with a fourth-and-one situation on our twenty-eight because they had the feeling that field goals weren't going to decide the issue that day.

We held them, or rather held their all-time rusher, Alex Webster, with a ten-man line. The next time the Giants scored only a half-minute of the game remained. In the meantime we had scored twenty-four points for an eventual 31–16 victory.

In a number of ways I rate 1959 one of the high spots of my pro career. I threw more TD passes that year (thirty-two) than in any other season. I kept my streak of touchdown-pass games going, and never threw less than two in a game in the regular season. In addition, there were a half-dozen games in which I threw three. We started the year by splitting the first two games. After that we won four in a row, lost to Washington and Cleveland, and finished up with five straight.

We had pretty much the identical personnel as we had in 1958, when rib injuries sidelined me for two games. We could count on plenty of running from Alan Ameche and Lenny Moore, and excellent receivers in Raymond Berry, Moore, and Jim Mutscheller. And we beat a fine Giant team again for the title. Throw out that last period and it was about as tough and exciting a game as you would want.

A couple of passes changed things around for us as the fourth period began. Berry caught one on a third-and-eight play to get us up around midfield, and then Lenny Moore cut inside Lindon Crow, one of the good Giant defensive backs, and got as far as the Giant thirteen before Dick Lynch grabbed him. Down at the three we tried a keeper and it worked. I rolled out to the right, Moore got in a key block, and I was into the end zone with our first score since Moore had taken a pass and had gone sixty yards for a touchdown in the first period.

That got us going. Andy Nelson intercepted one of

Charley Conerly's passes and took it down to the Giant fourteen. Two plays later I connected with Jerry Richardson in the end zone for another six points.

After that our defense assumed an increasingly important role. Johnny Sample intercepted a Conerly pass and ran half the distance of the field for the third Colt touchdown of the period. Another Sample interception set up a twenty-five-yard field goal by Steve Myhra, who found the pressure a lot less in this one than the previous year, where everything depended on his three points in the last seven seconds.

It's odd the things you remember about important games (and unimportant games, too), and the things you forget. For instance, some one reminded me recently that one of Pat Summerall's kicks—a thirty-six-yarder with a half-minute to go in the first half—was wide but that the officials had given it to him.

I don't even remember being aware of it, although the stories in the papers show that a fuss was made because a lot of newspapermen saw it and said that the official missed the call. They were sitting right behind the goal posts in the baseball press box. The regular football press box was jammed, and they constituted the overflow of a grand total of perhaps five hundred. (It's more at today's playoffs.)

The newspapermen screamed and hollered, but I guess their protests were drowned out in the general noise made by the fifty-seven thousand fans, most of them rooting for us. And after all, you have to be right behind the goal posts, watching the kicker, to be able to say definitely whether one is good or not. The newspapermen said "No" and the referee said "Yes," and you know who wins in those cases.

So we had back-to-back championships, something that doesn't happen too often, and we thought we were pretty good. Well, it *was* a pretty good record until Green Bay got going in the sixties.

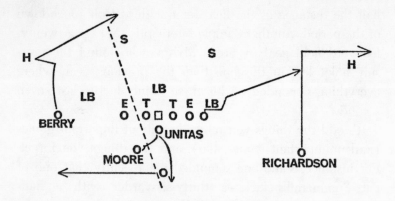

2. Typical Unitas–Berry Pass

Unitas fakes to the halfback (Moore) and throws to Berry, who runs a zig-out, zig-in pattern.

THE GAME: *Philadelphia vs. New York*
THE PLACE: *New York City*
THE TIME: *November 20, 1960*
FINAL SCORE: *Philadelphia, 17; New York, 10*

11. Toughest Eagle of Them All

When Vince Lombardi turned the Green Bay head coaching role over to Phil Bengtson in the winter of 1968, a good many had the mistaken notion that Lombardi had never lost a playoff. It was certainly a pardonable error because Vince had won so many, including those memorable three in a row from 1965 through 1967. He missed his first shot at the big prize, however, losing to a tough and talented Philadelphia club directed by Norm Van Brocklin and coached by Buck Shaw.

You could stick a pin into any letter of the alphabet and come up with the name of one or more outstanding ballplayers on that Philadelphia team. Take the "Bs" . . . Tom Brookshier, a defensive back; Don Burroughs, about as good a blitzing secondary as ever played; the hard-bitten Maxie Baughan, a linebacker, and Chuck Bednarik, the middle linebacker.

Bednarik was the last man in the pros to go two ways. He was an all-America at the University of Pennsylvania immediately after World War II and he played with the Eagles for fourteen years, setting what was probably a record for longtime occupancy of Franklin Field.

The Giants-Eagles rivalry has diminished in the past

decade, but at one time it was among the bitterest in
football. The Giants had a team doctor, Francis Sweeny,
who was able to provide a tart and appropriate comment
for most situations. He once summed up the feeling between
the Giants and Eagles: "Every time we play those fellows
we have to bring at least one of our players home through
the window."

This was the Doc's graphic method of describing the
handling of a stretcher case on a train. Railroad-car vesti-
bules were never constructed with the problems of four
men lugging a disabled football player in mind. It didn't
take long for football teams traveling by train to discover
that the easiest way to handle a stretcher was to move it
through a window and onto the platform.

The most famous single case of pure violence in the
history of the series involved Bednarik and Frank Gifford,
who has gone on to a successful career in TV after his
playing days were over. Thanks to an awesome collision
with Bednarik in late November of 1960, Gifford almost
had his career ended a couple of years early.

It took him out of action for a year, and when he
returned he did so in the role of a flanker, where contact
was negligible. His previous efforts as a ball carrier netted
him a lifetime mark of 3704 yards, second-highest in the
Giants' history.

Going back a bit to set the stage, Buck Shaw had taken
over the Eagles at a 4-8 low point in 1957. In 1958 Philadelphia managed only two victories, but Shaw got them
up to 7-5 in 1959. In 1960, after an opening loss to the
Browns, the Eagles won six in a row and suddenly realized
that they had a shot at the crown for the first time since
the Greasy Neale teams of the late forties.

Helping the Eagles' cause was the acquisition of Norm
Van Brocklin from the Rams a year or two earlier. The

incredibly agile Tommy McDonald was to grab thirteen TD passes from Van Brocklin that year, and there was Bednarik going two ways at the ripe age of thirty-five.

The big crash between Bednarik and Gifford took place in the 1960 game in Yankee Stadium at a time when the Giants were moving along with a 10–0 edge. During the first half the Giants had limited Philadelphia to a meager thirty-one yards in the rushing department, and Van Brocklin had been able to complete only one pass.

George Shaw was in as a replacement for the Giant quarterback, Charley Conerly, who was nursing a bad knee, and Shaw had set up Joe Morrison's TD plunge with a fifty-yard pass to Kyle Rote.

The other Giant points in the first half traced to Pat Summerall, a conversion and a twenty-six-yard field goal. Later, Pat was to have three tries in the second half and was to miss them all.

The Eagles trailed until the final five minutes of the game. They caught up on a Van Brocklin pass to McDonald and a short-distance field goal by Bobby Walston. The opportunity for the touchdown came on a fumbled handoff. Mel Triplett never got the ball cleanly, and when it popped into the air Jimmy Carr grabbed it and skittered thirty-six yards.

In the final three minutes, Shaw, blitzed and under heavy pressure, got off a pass to Gifford on the thirty. Burroughs nailed him with a low tackle. From the other side came Bednarik, charging high.

He hit Gifford like a semi-trailer. Down Frank went, the back of his helmeted head hitting the turf like a sack of concrete. The ball squirted from his slack arms, to be recovered by the Eagles on the thirty-six.

Other receivers have been knocked out, and a lot more are due for the same treatment, but what made this so different, was Bednarik's automatic reflex. He flung his arms toward the lowering skies in an unmistakable gesture of triumph. And it was immediately greeted by some of the worst booing ever heard in a Giants' home game.

Suddenly Chuck was not only aware that Gifford was down and out of the play but that he was going to remain that way. He dropped anxiously to his fallen opponent's side and then rose and remained motionless while the stretcher carried Gifford to the Giants' clubhouse.

Here another little drama-within-a-drama was enacted. They had laid Gifford on a trainer's table in the inner room of the clubhouse. There was a flurry as another stretcher was brought in. A special policeman was on it, apparently the victim of a heart attack. He was placed on the other table alongside Gifford. Just as the policeman died there, Gifford began to twitch his limbs. He had suffered a serious brain concussion.

Out on the field the Eagles had finished a successful job of killing the clock. They won 17–10, and if the Giants thought of avenging Frank the following week in a return match in Philadelphia they were mistaken, because there were eight points separating the two clubs in the rematch.

Gifford was hospitalized for a considerable length of time. The Giants used him as a scout and radio commentator in 1961 and he returned to help with the 1962 and 1963 Eastern titles as a flanker. He was one of the Giants' all-time favorites when he finished up after the 1964 season.

THE GAME: *Houston vs. San Diego*
THE PLACE: *San Diego*
THE TIME: *December 24, 1961*
FINAL SCORE: *Houston, 10; San Diego, 3*

12. Two in a Row for the Oilers

The Houston Oilers picked Billy Cannon, of L.S.U., in the first draft held by the American Football League, outbidding the Los Angeles Rams. They never regretted the move. Cannon stayed with the Oilers for four years before being traded to Oakland. In his first three years he appeared in as many championship playoffs, and he was voted most valuable player in the first two.

In both these games Houston beat the Chargers; in 1960 they were the Los Angeles Chargers, the following year they had switched to San Diego. Twice the Chargers had come out on top in the Western Division, only to run into the Oilers in the playoffs. And twice it was the passing combination of George Blanda and Billy Cannon that turned them back.

The second setback was tougher to take than the first for two reasons: It was played before a San Diego home crowd, and Cannon's touchdown was the only nonkicking score of the game. Playoff games are rarely gentlemanly, but the second San Diego-Houston contest was marked by 174 yards worth of penalties, plus the unusual scene of players being patched up on the sideline. Considering that the winners got seventeen hundred dollars a man and the losers one thousand dollars, it had to be one of the most intense title games ever played.

And that wasn't the only dramatic aspect. The year before Houston's victory had been directed by Lou Rymkus. He was a hometown hero—until the following October when he was fired with a 1-3-1 record and was replaced by Wally Lemm. The Oilers never lost another game that season, and climaxed the effort with a league championship. Lemm surprised a lot of people when he left the Oilers after the big victory, trading jobs with Pop Ivy of the St. Louis Cardinals. After a four-year interval, he returned to the Oilers for the 1966 season. In the meantime, Hall of Famer Sammy Baugh had replaced Pop Ivy, and Sammy had been replaced in turn by his assistant coach Bones Taylor, Sammy staying on as Taylor's assistant.

For a while you couldn't tell the coach without a program. Not only that, but it seemed the Oilers were constantly setting up housekeeping somewhere else. They moved from a high school field to Rice University's ample stadium, then for the 1968 season they became the first pro club to play on artificial turf, and faced the problem of supplying visiting teams with special footgear suitable for the Astrodome.

There wasn't too much scoring in the second Houston-Charger playoff. During the second quarter the Oilers got to the San Diego twenty-two but a Blanda pass intended for Billy Cannon was picked off in the end zone. Then a poor Charger punt gave Houston field position. Stopped on three downs, Blanda booted a forty-six-yard field goal. San Diego tried a three-pointer from just about the same distance shortly before the half, but missed.

In the third period Bud Whitehead, a defensive back, intercepted a first-down Blanda pass to head off a Houston threat on the Chargers' twenty-three. Halfway through the quarter San Diego was smacked with a fouling penalty and the Oilers took over on their own thirty-five. Little Charlie Tolar burst through to kick up a first down on the Charger forty. A pitchout to Cannon put it on the thirty-five.

On the next play the Chargers' front line forced Blanda out of the passing pocket. He rolled out and threw to Cannon, who was cutting across the field and just managed a leaping catch at the fifteen. Whitehead got a hand on him but was unable to stop the 212-pound Cannon. Bob McLeod, Houston's tight end, moved in for a final block and Billy crossed the line standing.

In a return bid the Chargers got to the Houston five on a fine run down the sideline by Bo Roberson, but had to settle for a twelve-yard field goal.

San Diego fought bitterly, knowing that a touchdown and a two-point conversion could do it, but they never got beyond the fifty. What finished them off was Julian Spence's interception of a Jack Kemp pass intended for big Dave Kocourek. Spence, at 153, was the lightest man in the league and had been brought back by Lemm after he had been cut earlier in the year. Kocourek, the fellow he took the ball away from, had a seventy-five-pound weight advantage.

Cannon was traded to Oakland in a three-for-one deal before the 1964 season. Al Davis used him as a running back for the Raiders, then realized that Billy's best running years were behind him. He switched him to the role of a tight end, and this move paid off in a series of successful seasons, climaxed by a 1967 effort of ten touchdowns in a championship game.

THE GAME: *Dallas vs. Houston*
THE PLACE: *Houston*
THE TIME: *December 23, 1962*
FINAL SCORE: *Dallas, 20; Houston, 17*

13. Football's Longest Day

The 1962 American Football League championship game was unusual on several counts. First, it was the longest major-league game ever played—seventeen minutes and fifty-four seconds' worth of sudden death. Second, it was the last major-league title game played in a high school stadium. And last, it was the only time that a team ever won a championship and left town. The 1962 Dallas Texans became the Kansas City Chiefs in 1963.

There have been other moves by clubs successful on the field but a little slow at the box office. In the NFL the Boston Redskins of the late thirties became the Washington Redskins, and their owner, George Marshall, was so mad at the Boston noncustomers that he took the 1936 championship game to New York (where he lost to the Packers). A couple of years before the Texans won the AFL crown, the Los Angeles Chargers won the Western title, lost to Houston in the title game, and promptly moved to San Diego.

Dallas and Houston were by far the two best ball clubs in the AFL in 1962. Each had 11-3 records. The only other clubs in the league with winning records were Boston (9-4-1) and Buffalo (7-6-1). Frank (Pop) Ivy was the third Houston coach in as many years; Dallas had Hank Stram at the helm, in the early stages of what was to prove a record-breaking tenure as a head coach in the league.

Both clubs had sound personnel. George Blanda, the Oilers' quarterback, who had seen championship action with the 1956 Chicago Bears, also represented the Oilers' No. 1 scoring threat with his kicking. Dallas was directed by Lenny Dawson, who was to become the first AFL quarterback in the Super Bowl.

Dallas's kicking was the responsibility of Tommy Brooker, a first-year performer from Demopolis, Alabama. He kicked a sixteen-yard field goal to open the scoring in the first quarter, and a few hours later he ended the game with a twenty-five-yarder in semi-darkness.

Dallas played the first half as though they wanted to get the game over as quickly as possible. With Chris Burford out of action, Hank Stram had moved Abner Haynes into the flanker spot, and played with two tight ends. Haynes' running role in the first half was entrusted to Jack Spikes, who had been out with an injury early in the year and had fooled a lot of people when he was re-activated late in the season. Spikes wound up winning Most Valuable Player honors for the game.

The Texans had a 17–0 edge at the half, thanks to Brooker's kick and a couple of scores by Haynes. One came on a twenty-eight-yard pass from Dawson, the other on a two-yard run. Things looked pretty bleak for Houston.

But the second half was a complete reversal. The Oilers permitted Dallas out of its own end of the field only once. They scored the first time they got the ball, on a fifteen-yard Blanda pass to Willard Dewveall. Blanda kicked a thirty-one-yard field goal, then Charlie Tolar blasted across from the one and the score was tied. Blanda tried another field goal from the thirty-one but it was blocked by Sherrill Headrick, the linebacker. "It would have been good," said George later. The three points would also have meant the difference.

The overtime was the first since the Colts had beaten the Giants in the 1958 NFL championship. This one was going to take a little longer. It was also to have a slightly erratic start.

There was a coin toss to determine who would kick off. Dallas wasn't too confident about its punting. They figured that if Houston were forced to punt Dallas would ultimately have better field position. Hank Stram, the Dallas coach, assumed Houston would want to receive if they won the toss, so he instructed Haynes to make certain that Dallas would be defending the goal with the wind at their back. If Dallas won, Haynes was also to ask for the wind, letting Houston choose to receive.

When the coin came up the way Haynes called it, he became confused. "We'll kick to the clock," he said, meaning with the wind behind him.

"You can't have both," explained the referee. "It's either the kick or the wind."

"We'll kick off," said Haynes, while the TV cameras panned to show the consternation which ran through the Dallas coaching staff as Houston lined up with the wind at its back.

The eventual Dallas victory took Abner off a large hook. Instead it was Blanda who absorbed most of the blame. Twice in the overtime he was intercepted, and the second one led to the deciding score. Bill Hull, a defensive end, picked off a pass intended for Charley Hennigan on his own thirty and returned it to midfield. There was one short Dallas gain before the fifth quarter ended and the teams switched. Now the Texans had the wind at their backs.

Dawson hit Spikes with a ten-yard pass, then sent him around the weak side on a third-and-six effort for nineteen yards. "The linebacker on the strong side was 'cheating' a little," said Dawson later, "so we took a chance and it worked."

On the next three downs, Dallas gained only one yard. Brooker then stepped back and booted one from the twenty-five. "They had to tell me whether it was good or not," he said. "I was too scared to look up from the ground."

THE GAME: *Green Bay vs. New York*
THE PLACE: *New York City*
THE TIME: *December 30, 1962*
FINAL SCORE: *Green Bay, 16; New York, 7*

14. It's Drafty, Someone Please Shut the Door

New York's weather, like its skyline, is remarkable. Fifty-degree variations over a twenty-four-hour period are no novelty. When it's spring at midnight and howling winter the following morning, and particularly if the morning is that of a championship football game, it makes for an interesting afternoon. And the 1962 championship contest between the Green Bay Packers and the New York Giants was to prove one of the more interesting of the NFL's playoffs.

It had rained the previous evening. By the time the last bistro closed, sending the visitors back to their hotels for a few hours' sleep before the game, a noticeable spring-like breeze had sprung up.

The Giants were pleased at the prospect that the wind would dry out the field. This would favor them slightly because Y. A. Tittle was rated an edge over Bart Starr as a pin-point passer.

But what was a mere post-midnight breeze gathered force toward dawn. When the crowds started toward Yankee Stadium at midmorning they found they had to lean into the wind. And somewhere along the line the thermometer had lost about thirty degrees' worth of temperature. Fans who had the foresight to bring big parkas and muk-luks were lucky. The rest suffered almost as much as the players. At one point a radio announcer went to take a drink of what he thought was hot coffee and had his lip freeze to the rim of the cup.

There are those who insist that weather conditions sometimes make a mockery of talent in a football game, and maybe they're right. Perhaps every championship game should be played in a mild, sunny climate. Or, if the game must be played in the home city of one of the two teams involved, what's wrong with postponing it a day for a better break in the weather?

Well, in this case the next day would have been worse, and the day after that worse yet. The wind blew with near-hurricane strength for three days, lifting roofs, rolling large cement blocks, and toppling chimneys in New York and its surrounding area. And through it all, the sun smiled as though it were a dandy day for the beach.

This was before the days of "wind-chill factor," now so popular on TV weather reports . . . take the temperature and add the force of the wind and come up with what it feels like . . . twenty below if the temperature is ten and there is a thirty-mile-an-hour wind blowing.

It was the second straight championship game between New York and Green Bay. The previous year they had played in Green Bay, where such weather can be expected. The Giants weren't quite prepared for Paul Hornung's nineteen-points effort that day, still a championship game record, and were soundly beaten, 37–0. Now they were back with a tough, skilled defense and they were playing at home, in the same park in which they had won the title six years earlier.

Games are usually won on the other club's mistakes, and the seasoned Giant defense didn't plan to make many.

Green Bay didn't plan to make many, either, but when they did they got lucky. The Packers fumbled five times and recovered each time.

The Packers had Jim Taylor, who was the league's leading rusher that year with 1474 yards and nineteen touchdowns. A lot depended on the Giants' ability to stop Taylor.

Bart Starr, the Green Bay quarterback, gave the ball to Taylor thirty-one times, and Taylor absorbed almost unendurable punishment. The Giant defense waited for him. It knew he had to come up the middle because the footing made any running to the outside virtually impossible. To add to Taylor's troubles, he bit his tongue badly early in the game and kept swallowing blood all day.

Taylor had to run against a defensive front four of Andy Robustelli, Rosey Grier, Dick Modzelewski, and Jim Katcavage, with Sam Huff plugging the hole in the middle. This group had played as a unit for seven seasons. It was given to few miscues.

In the second quarter, though, with the Packers leading on the first of Jerry Kramer's three successful field goals, the Giants erred. It was on the Packers' best power play, a fullback slant off right tackle. Huff, reading the play correctly when Taylor took one step to the right, vacated the middle, moving to shut off the hole. That put four Giants in the off-tackle slot, Huff, Katcavage, Modzelewski, and Bill Winter, the outside linebacker. Taylor saw the middle wide open. He just tiptoed back over center on the frozen ground (they all wore corrugated-sole shoes) and scored.

It was the only play in which the Giants failed to touch him. "They made up for it the rest of the game," Taylor recalled grimly.

In the third quarter Erich Barnes, a Giant defensive back,

blocked a punt and Jim Collier, a substitute end, fell on it for a touchdown. That was the first and last time the Giants were to score. Kramer later kicked his second and third field goals, one from the twenty-nine, the other from the thirty. He missed two of five that day, remarkable in the light of the game conditions.

The 16–7 victory was another of several peaks in the coaching career of Vincent Lombardi. The year before he had won his first playoff title. Now he had one in his own hometown. Later there were to be the three in a row, and two Super Bowl triumphs.

As Lombardi's semi-frozen players hoisted him onto their shoulders, the writers took pencils in congealed fingers to vote for the game's Most Valuable Player, a distinction that carried with it a complimentary sports car. There were three candidates—Taylor, who had displayed almost superhuman endurance; Kramer, whose kicking had proved the difference; and Ray Nitschke, the middle linebacker. For the first time the award went to a linebacker (it was to go to another the following year, the Bears' Larry Morris).

Nitschke had played a memorable game. He had plugged up the middle, confining the Giants' big runners, Alex Webster and Phil King. And he had contributed two vital "turn-arounds," invaluable when ball clubs are so evenly matched.

In the first quarter Tittle had pegged one to Joe Walton, frantically wigwagging in the end zone. Nitschke deflected the ball so that Bill Currie, another linebacker, was able to grab it and take it to midfield. In the third quarter, after the Giants had scored to get back into the running, they fumbled a Green Bay punt. Nitschke was right there to recover it.

Later, Tittle was to pay tribute to the Packers as a

team of perfect defense. He pointed out Henry Jordan, the tackle, as a pass rusher with abilities usually reserved for the more agile ends. Nitschke he described as the vital figure in the linebacking.

Said Tittle: "Their defense was as good as ours and their running was better. But I'd like to play them again on our kind of a day when I could let a pass go without wondering where the wind was going to take it. I guess we'll never know now."

THE GAME: *New York vs. Cleveland*
THE PLACE: *Cleveland*
THE TIME: *October 27, 1963*
FINAL SCORE: *New York, 33; Cleveland, 6*

15. The Day Everything Worked

Jim Brown gained an unprecedented 1863 yards during the 1963 season. His total was equal to the combined efforts of the next two men, a staggering thought when you realize that the second-best rusher that year was Green Bay's Jim Taylor, with more than one thousand yards.

Yet, oddly enough, Brown had one of his poorest days ever during that season. It came against the New York Giants before a home crowd of 84,213 in Cleveland's cavernous Municipal Stadium. On that day three Giant runners outrushed Brown, who carried for a meager forty yards in nine tries. Moreover, Jim was ejected for fighting in the dying moments of the game, a rare occurrence for him.

Two weeks earlier, in Yankee Stadium, Brown had had a picnic against this same Giant club. He had scored three touchdowns, and had wrung reluctant admiration from the Giant fans with scoring runs of seventy-two and thirty-two yards. The seventy-two-yarder was a screen pass, where Brown turned on some of his speed to shake or outrun various members of the Giants' swift, talented secondary. The 35–24 Cleveland victory in that contest had put the Browns two games ahead in the Eastern race. There seemed scant hope of the Giants, or anyone else, catching them.

Before the rematch, the Giants were scheduled to face the Cowboys. They had had a reasonably tough time with Dallas and their five-seven quarterback, Eddie LeBaron, who held the distinction of being the only practicing lawyer in pro football. After trailing in the first half the Giants had gotten to little Eddie in the second, administering a pretty good thumping. But no one was predicting any kind of a Giant upset for the following week in Cleveland.

Later, Allie Sherman, the Giants' coach, was to call this the best game any of his Giant clubs ever played, in the matter of execution. "We made only two mistakes in the entire game," he advised newsmen after a momentous 33–6 triumph, which hauled the Giants back into the middle of what was to prove a winning race.

Sherman never did explain what those two mistakes were. Which was just as well, because all players are human. If one makes a mistake this week, chances are it will be someone else the next.

Accompanying the near-flawless execution was a charged-up defense which took the momentum away from the Browns completely. On the third play of the game John LoVetere, a hefty tackle, hit Jim Brown hard enough to cause him to fumble. Sam Huff, one of the few men near Brown's equal in a one-on-one situation, recovered on the thirty, and Don Chandler kicked a twenty-nine-yard field goal.

On the next Cleveland offensive play, Frank Ryan's pass to John Brewer was intercepted by Jim Patton. Tittle hit Del Shofner with a touchdown pass from the twenty-two, and the Giants were ahead 10–0 before a fair portion of the enormous crowd had even found seats.

It was 17–0 at the quarter and 23–0 at the half. The Giants had scored every time they got the ball. The carnage continued when play resumed. Don Chandler kicked another field goal, Tittle directed another scoring drive, and now it was seven times getting the ball, and seven times scoring with it! With a quarter to go, the margin had stretched to 33–0.

Frank Ryan, who was a mathematics scholar, might have had some trouble toting up a grocery list after the shellacking he took from the Giant defense. When Larry Benz managed to intercept a Tittle-to-Frank-Gifford pass, Jim Ninowski replaced Ryan and directed the Browns to what was to be their only touchdown. The key plays were a pair of passes, one to Tom Hutchinson, the other a short peg over the middle to Rich Kreiting for the touchdown.

The score came just when the Browns' research division, upstairs in the press box, had unearthed the statistic that a shutout for Cleveland would be the first in 162 games.

Sherman decided that a 33–6 margin with two minutes to go was safe enough, so he inserted young Glynn Griffing at quarterback. A punt gave the ball to the Browns and in the next sequence Jim Brown and the Giants' outside linebacker, Tom Scott, got to swinging and were tossed out.

The unexpected victory was exactly what the Giants needed to spark their second-half drive. It left them a game behind the Browns with seven to play, but now the New Yorkers were convinced that no man is invincible every Sunday of the season, and that they were a better team than even they themselves had realized. The Giants went on to win six of their next seven games, good enough to take the title. The Browns managed only four victories during the remainder of the season.

THE GAME: *Buffalo vs. New York*
THE PLACE: *Buffalo*
THE TIME: *December 8, 1963*
FINAL SCORE: *Buffalo, 45; New York, 14*

16. Cookie's Biggest Day

No one can even begin to estimate what sort of niche Cookie Gilchrist might have carved for himself had he played his entire career in the major leagues. He didn't appear on the American scene until 1962, when he was signed as a free agent after eight seasons of Canadian football. He had started playing as a nineteen-year-old and didn't burst upon the American sporting public until he was in his late twenties.

He left an indelible mark, though, before he finally finished up in 1967. He reached the thousand-yard level in 1962, and produced a 243-yard game in 1963. That is not the most rushing yardage ever rolled up in a major-league contest, but it is tops for either an American or National Football League game. Orban (Spec) Sanders still holds the record with his 250 yards in twenty-four carries for the New York Yankees in the All-America Conference.

Cookie was a large, vocal man who left little doubt in anyone's mind where he stood on any particular issue. He never complained no matter how many times he was given the ball (he carried three dozen times on his biggest day). Only when they looked elsewhere for someone to run with the ball did Cookie object.

The 1963 American League schedule kept Buffalo and New York apart until the last couple of weeks of the season, then threw them together in home-and-home games on successive weeks. The first game was played in Buffalo's Memorial Stadium, and despite New York's last-place standing in the Eastern Division, the Titans were given a fairly good chance. Buffalo, unhappy with Jack Kemp's work at quarterback, had benched him for rookie Daryle Lamonica. The Titans had not given up a touchdown in their last two games and had an experienced, if unspectacular, club.

On the very first play from scrimmage Dick Wood was thrown for a loss attempting to pass and was less than successful in getting back on his feet. He had strained a ligament in his knee. It didn't make any difference which one because Wood was the surgery champ at the time with three operations on one and two on the other.

When Buffalo took over, Lamonica got good results by giving Gilchrist the ball, and saw no reason to change. Cookie carried eight of the first nine times. He scored a touchdown in the first period and another in the second. Lamonica also threw a TD pass to Elbert Dubenion in the second period, and at halftime the score was 24–7.

When play continued, Gilchrist kept plugging away at the Titan defenses, all 250 pounds of him. Finally Buffalo's coach, Lou Saban, figured he had enough points and Cookie had had enough work for the day. When Buffalo took the field after a turnover, there was someone else in Cookie's fullback spot.

After two plays the sideline phone rang. It was the Buffalo coach assigned to spot from a booth adjoining the press box. "Hey," he told Saban excitedly, "the guys up here are yelling bloody murder. They say Gilchrist is thirty-one yards short of the record. Maybe you'd better put him back in." The AFL record was 216 yards. It had been set two years earlier by Billy Cannon, of Houston, against the same New York Club.

Back Cookie went, and he was just as effective in the waning moments as he had been at the outset. There was high excitement among the writers once he had passed Cannon's mark. The next was Jim Brown's pro record of 237, which the great Cleveland fullback had achieved twice. That went, too. By the end of the game, Cookie had 243 yards and five touchdowns, on runs ranging from one to nineteen yards.

The postgame statistics made some entertaining reading. Cookie had outrushed the entire Titans' team, 243 to 38. He had carried the ball more than twice as many times as all the Titan runners combined.

Buffalo went down to New York and beat the Titans again the following week. Eventually they got into a divisional playoff with Boston, which they lost. Cookie was the rushing leader in the American League the next year

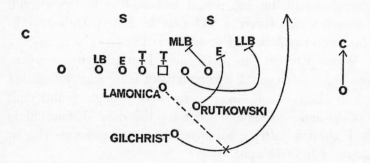

3. Cookie Gilchrist Takes Pitchout around Right End

Rutkowski fakes into the line, where he blocks out the defensive left end. The right tackle blocks down on the middle linebacker (MLB). The right guard pulls and blocks the left linebacker (LLB).

and got into the playoff, where he picked up 122 yards against San Diego.

Buffalo traded him to Denver that winter for a player of lesser talents. Cookie had been at Buffalo for three seasons, and that had always been the limit for any of his stays. Before he finished up he played for both Denver and Miami, then retired to oversee his many interests, ranging from a gold mine in Canada to a maid service in Denver.

THE GAME: *Chicago vs. New York*
THE PLACE: *Chicago*
THE TIME: *December 29, 1963*
FINAL SCORE: *Chicago, 14; New York, 10*

17. Y.A.'s Last Big Game

The year I came to Baltimore, 1956, was the last year in which the New York Giants won the championship. They won eight of their twelve games (there was a tie in there), and then beat Chicago pretty much as they pleased on a cold, raw December afternoon in Yankee Stadium. The final score was 47–7. These clubs had played a 17–17 tie a month earlier, and after the title game the Giants were wondering whether this was really the same club.

We beat the Giants in 1958 and 1959, and they had three more shots at the championship in the early sixties without making it. They lost to Green Bay in 1961 and 1962. In 1963 the Bears, who lost one less game than Green Bay did that year, took the Giants in the title game in a glacial setting at Wrigley Field.

To my way of thinking the 1963 Giants were one of the more interesting teams they've put on the field in their half-century history. They matched each situation as it developed, overcoming a halftime deficit of 21–3 against us in the opening game, to race through the season, and beat Pittsburgh in the final game. A Pittsburgh victory would have given the Steelers the Eastern Conference championship, even though they had won only seven games to the Giants' ten (the Steelers had three ties and these didn't affect the percentages).

At any rate 1963 was Y. A. Tittle's biggest year. He threw thirty-six touchdown passes, a league record which still stands. He was hurt badly in the first game, and a knee injury in the playoff destroyed his effectiveness when he was almost within viewing distance of the championship. The playoff injury was to take its toll the following year, his last.

Chicago also had an unusual team that year. The previous season the Bears had managed a third-place finish in the West on a 9-5 record. Most of the other clubs rated them a bunch of has-beens, coached by a man who was one of the game's immortals but perhaps a little past his prime. We had no way of knowing that George Halas was to institute one of the great defensive games in training that July at St. Joseph's College in Rensselaer, Indiana, and use it to win the title even though there were nine other clubs in the league who scored more points than the Bears did.

The way it worked out, the Giants played the Bears twice that year, the first time in the opening preseason game at Cornell University's picturesque stadium in Ithaca, New York.

There was nothing picturesque about the Bears that preseason weekend. They were all grim business. Smarting at the insinuation that the parade had passed him by, and at such cracks from the opposition as, "We knew what play was coming two plays ahead," Halas had put the whip to his boys in training camp. The Giants were staying in the dormitories at Cornell, and when they went into town that evening to see a movie they were a little surprised not to find a single Bear on the streets—or anywhere else.

Halas had locked them all in for the night at Ithaca

College, where he ordered everyone to be in bed by ten. The Bears were still steaming when they showed up at three o'clock the following afternoon for the game.

The Giants went after the Bears in a hurry and were a little surprised to come up with a clawed nose. At the half the Bears were not only in front but were looking for trouble. They found it on the final play before intermission.

A Bears' sideliner who didn't care for the action on an out-of-bounds play swung his idle helmet at the recumbent Giant runner. That set things off. From the opposite side of the field Allie Sherman watched, confident that old Poppa Bear would calm everyone down. Instead, to his amazement, Halas entered the battle himself, getting in a few judicious shots.

Allie scampered across the field, grabbed Halas, and yelled, "For crying out loud, George, it's not even a regular-season game! What are you getting all worked up for?" Ken Kavanaugh and Ed Colman, two ex-Bears who were coaching for Sherman, helped quiet down their old boss, who eventually left the premises that day reasonably satisfied with a 17–7 victory.

Five months later the two teams met again. The Giants had the best offensive club in the league. Tittle had enjoyed a phenomenal year and his favorite receiver, a skinny Texan named Del Shofner, had caught sixty-four passes, including nine for touchdowns. There were other standouts, too, like Frank Gifford, Joe Morrison, and big Phil King coming out of the backfield.

There weren't too many Bears left from the 1956 team that had taken such a bad beating from the Giants, but the handful of holdovers really had to appreciate what happened that frozen afternoon. Tittle was intercepted five times, twice on screen passes. He had been intercepted only fourteen times all year. Five times in a game was a record for him, in New York, San Francisco, or anywhere else.

The Bears also blanked Shofner, and in that connection they may have had a little unwitting help from a newspaperman who wrote a trumped-up story because of his paper's insistence on a catchy headline. In the middle of the week before the big game, with just about everything already said, the reporter still had to come up with something that would cause Christmas shoppers to stop and look at the big, black type. He wrote a story which could be described as "hypothetical" only by stretching charity to the utmost. He posed it as a question: Shofner for Hornung? meaning a one-for-one trade between New York and Green Bay. And that's the way the headline read.

The team saw the story when it got on the charter flight for Chicago. The high-strung Shofner immediately figured that where there was large black type there was some basis of fact. No amount of assurance from Sherman, or any of the other coaches, could quite convince him. It unquestionably affected his outlook for the rest of the week and probably influenced his play during the game, in which Tittle threw him five passes and never connected with any.

Sherman fumed over the story. He announced on the plane, "Shofner for Hornung? I wouldn't make that trade even if they threw in Hornung's 'little black book,'" a reference to the Golden Boy's active social life.

From the back of the place came a voice which could easily have belonged to the formidable defensive tackle, Dick Modzelewski, "Not so fast, coach."

The championship game was the first played in Wrigley Field in a couple of decades. The Giants scored in the opening period on a Tittle pass to Gifford. Then Billy

Wade, the Bears' quarterback, evened things up by taking the ball over from the two.

In the second period Don Chandler kicked a field goal, giving New York a 10–7 lead at the half. But before it ended the Giants knew they were in plenty of trouble. The Bears hadn't been able to prevent Y.A. from throwing a TD pass on a zig-out pattern, but as Tittle was unloading the ball he was hit across the left leg by the blitzing linebacker, Larry Morris.

Then late in the second period, as Tittle slipped on the frozen turf, Morris, who was to be chosen the game's Most Valuable Player, came shooting in again. Again he made contact with Tittle's left knee. This time the pain shot clear up Y.A.'s leg. He could hardly limp off the field to permit Glynn Griffing to finish up the half.

They shot him with cortisone and Novocain during the intermission and he went back in. Allie Sherman asked him whether he thought he could make it. If Allie expected any answer other than "Yes," he was talking to the wrong player. Tittle had played at various times in his career with two sprained ankles, a broken cheekbone, a broken hand, and a bad back. A bum knee, in what was to prove his last bid for a championship, wasn't going to stop him.

But the Bears, well aware of Tittle's injury, were not about to be stopped, either. Shortly after the second half began Tittle missed an easy one to Frank Gifford on a sideline square out. Gifford was wide open, waiting, but the pass came late. And for a very good reason. Y.A. simply couldn't plant his front leg, the injured one, to throw properly.

The next time Tittle threw, the pass was intended for Shofner and it was intercepted. The Giants survived this mishap, but later in the period Tittle tried a screen pass to the right. Ed O'Bradovich, the end, intercepted and ran it from the Giants' thirty-eight to the thirteen. Ultimately Wade went in with it again. Halas later termed O'Bradovich's interception the turning point of the game.

Tittle was still putting the ball in the air when the game-ending gun sounded and the customers got to their feet only to realize they'd be walking to their parked cars on frozen stumps. With 1:40 to go, Tittle threw eight passes, completed four (the Bears were giving him the short stuff), missed with one, threw two away, and had the last one intercepted by Richie Petitbon in the end zone.

Thus Tittle's biggest year ended on a note of frustration. He was the leading passer in the league and he won the Most Valuable Player award, but the Bears took away his final shot at the biggest prize a quarterback can aim for.

What they couldn't take away, however, was his mark of three dozen TD passes in a season. No one has been able to touch it since.

THE GAME: *Cleveland vs. St. Louis*
THE PLACE: *St. Louis*
THE TIME: *December 6, 1964*
FINAL SCORE: *St. Louis, 28; Cleveland, 19*

18. The Redbirds Fly High

The 1964 race in the National League's Eastern Conference
was one of the tighter ones, in contrast to our conference,
where Baltimore sewed it up early. Most teams like it that
way—the early wrapup for you and the tough stretch drive
for the other club so that when you meet in the playoff
you're completely rested and the other fellow is still pant-
ing. Naturally, sometimes it works and sometimes it
doesn't.

The Cards' bid in 1964 was the best they had put on
since they moved to St. Louis, leaving Chicago a one-team
city. They took it down to the final week of the season,
chasing the Browns, whom they had played to a tie early
in the season, and upsetting them in the next-to-last game.
A half-game in front, the Browns had to win their last
one against the Giants. Then no matter what St. Louis did,
the Browns would have the title.

And that's the way it turned out. The Browns' quarterback, Frank Ryan, enjoyed an almost incredible afternoon against the Giants, completing twelve passes in thirteen attempts with five of the completions resulting in
touchdowns. He spread them generously among such performers as Paul Warfield, Gary Collins, Ernie Green, and

Jimmy Brown. The game was on Saturday afternoon TV and we watched rather closely because this was to be the team we would play in the championship two weeks later. Apparently, we didn't watch as closely as we thought we had.

Anyone who saw the Browns fail to get started in St. Louis would have been justified in underestimating them. Charlie Johnson, the Cards' quarterback, passed for a couple of touchdowns and scored twice himself. The Cardinal defense held Jimmy Brown to sixty-eight yards in fourteen carries. Four field goals by Lou Groza, the greatest scorer of them all, added up to more than half of Cleveland's total.

Johnson was one of the busier quarterbacks in pro ball in the early sixties. He was doing graduate work in chemical engineering at Washington University in St. Louis in addition to quarterbacking a major-league team, no mean feat. In 1963 he set a Cardinal record with twenty-eight touchdowns. There is excellent evidence that the shoulder injury he sustained early in 1965 influenced his career. In 1967 he entered the Army as a reserve officer, and the Cardinals' front office turned to younger aspirants.

But on that cold December afternoon in the old St. Louis ball park, Johnson came through with an outstanding performance. The Browns got off in front with the first of Lou Groza's field goals, but Johnson opened up in the second period, hitting the fullback, Joe Childress, with a forty-six-yard touchdown pass. Childress went through the middle, caught the ball on the Browns' twenty-six, and outran the secondary.

On the first play from scrimmage after the TD Larry Stallings, a St. Louis linebacker, intercepted and returned the ball a dozen yards to the Cleveland twenty-six. The interception had been set up by Luke Owens, a defensive lineman, who had nailed Ryan as he was attempting to pass, causing him to get off a wobbly toss.

Two running plays by John David Crow and two pass completions brought the ball down to the one, and Johnson took it in. Later in the same period Johnson threw another touchdown pass, this one to Bobby Joe Conrad. The best Cleveland could manage in the closing moments of the first half was a second field goal by Groza.

Groza kicked another field goal early in the third period, but his next effort was blocked and St. Louis turned it into a touchdown march at the end of which Johnson scored a second time.

The Browns, struggling to catch up in the final period, scored with a field goal and a touchdown pass from Ryan to Ernie Green, but then time ran out on them.

The following Saturday Cleveland defeated the Giants to clinch the title. Unfortunately for the Colts, the momentum carried into the playoff, where a nearly perfect defensive game enabled the Browns to fashion a rare playoff shutout over us.

THE GAME: *Baltimore vs. Cleveland*
THE PLACE: *Cleveland*
THE TIME: *December 27, 1964*
FINAL SCORE: *Cleveland, 27; Baltimore, 0*

19. One of My Lesser Afternoons

There have to be worse things than seeing your favorite team victimized by someone else's perfect game. Name one? Well, being in such a game on the losing side, for instance, as I was in the 1964 championship.

We had been the best-scoring club in the National League that year (428 points), and we had also been the toughest on defense (225 points). We had it all wrapped up a couple of weeks from the end, while the Browns had to go down to the last weekend. What happened in the playoff was merely further proof that anything can happen when the stakes are high and a team rises to the challenge with near-perfect execution.

There was no reason for our being terribly concerned about the Browns that weekend in Cleveland while we waited for our first try at the NFL title since 1959. We all knew that Jim Brown was the best runner in the business and that Frank Ryan had thrown five touchdown passes the previous week in just a dozen completions. But we had Lenny Moore finishing up a year in which he had broken Jim Taylor's single-season touchdown record (twenty). We had Raymond Berry, who had boosted his lifetime total to 506 passes, to top Jim Howton's previous mark. And while I had thrown only nineteen touchdown passes (a little under my average), I had been intercepted only six times.

We stayed at the Sheraton-Cleveland Hotel along with a large delegation of Colt supporters, and we spent some of Saturday afternoon watching Buffalo beat San Diego on TV for the American League title. It was a freakish day over in Buffalo. The temperature there was nearly fifty. The grass was slick and lights were needed because of a heavy haze. Buffalo is to the east. Weather travels from Cleveland to Buffalo, not the other way around, so what we got next day was a windy, overcast afternoon, with temperatures just a notch or two above freezing.

This was Don Shula's second year with us as head coach and we wanted to win for him just a little more than we would ordinarily. Don had been a defensive back with the Browns before going into coaching. He was also a local boy. He came from Painesville, which was just down the road from the stadium on the lakefront.

We went in there trying to run and throw, mixing it up as much as possible, and hoping we could neutralize Jim Brown enough to make them put it into the air where our fellows might have a chance to pick one off. As it turned out, it was just about the other way around.

Cleveland's linebackers played a tremendous game. Every time I went back to throw they'd have such quick position on our receivers that you just couldn't put the ball into the air without risking an interception. I knew I was in for an interesting afternoon when I was thrown for a loss twice within the first half-dozen attempts while looking for a receiver.

Their defensive linemen handled our pass blockers with ease. Rarely did I have the luxury of being able to look around for a second receiver. Surprisingly, our defense played on a level close to Cleveland's, and the first half wound up scoreless.

Early in the second half, in fact during the first series of downs on which we had the ball, the game could have turned around on one play. With the kind of coverage the Browns were plastering on our receivers, I figured I'd try a screen pass to Moore. Given a step or so, Lenny was as fast and as elusive as anyone.

I hit him with one and he started to run. Our linemen had knocked down just about everyone but Galen Fiss, the outside linebacker who was on Moore's side of the field. We had a blocker out in front of Moore but Fiss came through and grabbed Lennie by the shoe.

What are the odds on someone making a tackle like that? The shoe, the hand, and everything else, have to be in the right spot at the right time. Down went Lennie. If Fiss had not made that last-ditch tackle, Lennie would have gone all the way. We'd have been out front, and who knows whether the Browns could have generated any comeback momentum? It's a peculiar commodity, especially in championship games.

But with this kind of a break Cleveland went right to work again. Again I was faced with the most formidable pass defense of the year. Never once was I able to take my first choice among the receivers. Frankly I rate it one of the worst days I ever had as a passer. I looked up my figures for that day recently. They were less than one hundred yards.

Brown? He ran well but not sensationally. He didn't have to. His 114 yards in 27 attempts gave Frank Ryan just the right proportion of running and passing in his attack. Ryan hit Gary Collins with three touchdown passes, helped in no small measure by the indifferent punting we had that day. There was a pretty good breeze coming in off the lake, as I remember, which cut down on the yard-age. But I remember, too, that their punter, Collins, had to kick into the same wind and had no particular problems.

So the Browns took some eight thousand dollars per man as the winning share and we came up with fifty-five hundred dollars. Jim Brown put the cap on another big year, and that winter picked up the Hickok Belt, which is the Pro Athlete of the Year award, and is valued at ten thousand dollars.

That was the last we saw of Jim Brown because Cleveland wasn't on our 1965 schedule and he retired shortly before the start of training in 1966.

Elsewhere I've indicated that he was the best runner I have seen, though the book isn't closed yet on Gale Sayers. We didn't play the Browns too often because we are in different conferences of the NFL, but I recall a five-touchdown afternoon Brown had against us in 1958. And we've studied a lot of Brown's films and a lot of his record yardage.

For sheer strength and intelligence you couldn't beat Jim. On that five-touchdown day against us, for instance, we had keys on him, in other words we knew which way he was going to go, right or left. We could read him, so I guess the other teams in the league could, too.

Normally it isn't too easy, but the Browns didn't seem to care much whether you knew or not.

How did we do it? Well, if he were going to the right he'd have one hand down, if it were to be to the left he'd have the other hand down. It was as simple as that, but try to stop him. He was a great runner, and most of the time he had very good people in front of him.

Brown never "forced" anything. Seldom did you see Jim lower his head or shoulder on someone. If he went up to the line of scrimmage and hit in there and there was nothing, he would slide right down the line until he found a hole. It seemed to be a kind of sixth sense with him.

Jim ran with his head up. A lot of runners duck as soon as they get the ball, but you could always see Brown's eyes. He was always looking. He never tried to run over anyone like a Jim Taylor, who will go out of his way to try to run over the top of you. Taylor used to say he liked to "sting" the tacklers a little.

Brown was a thinker on the field, and he lasted longer than he would have if he had just smashed into everyone, because they ran him a great deal. Check the record book and you'll find that the first three "most attempts one season" belong to Jim—305 in 1961, 291 in 1963, and 290 in 1959. In 1963 he set the season record of 1863 yards, and his career mark is four thousand yards better than his closest competitor.

On the other hand Brown was just as strong sliding off for a second effort as most runners are in their first crack. I heard Gino Marchetti, our defensive end, once say that

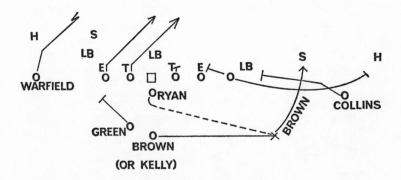

4. Typical Cleveland Browns' Pitchout

The Browns' "money" running play, used so successfully first with Jim Brown and later with Leroy Kelly. Invariably it is run to the strong side.

if you tackled him and didn't get a good hold, Jim was liable to tear your fingers right out of their sockets.

He had more thousand-yard seasons than anyone else, and seemed virtually immune to physical punishment. Actually there were some pretty big men who hit him squarely over the years. He simply didn't show it. He suffered an injury to a big toe early in one of his best seasons and balked at having it treated. No one ever knew the extent of the injury, but it is quite likely that Jim Brown was the leading rusher that year—on a broken toe.

THE GAME: *Green Bay vs. Baltimore*
THE PLACE: *Baltimore*
THE TIME: *December 12, 1965*
FINAL SCORE: *Green Bay, 42; Baltimore, 27*

20. Paul Leaves 'Em Smiling

No book on pro football could possibly be complete without a bow to Paul Hornung, the highest scorer, and one of the most dynamic players in the game's history. For a decade Paul dominated headlines. He helped the Packers move from a last-place club to one that won four NFL titles. In 1960 he set an almost unbelievable record of 176 points for a single season. And that year we played twelve-game schedules, too.

Paul was originally a quarterback out of Notre Dame, and went to Green Bay as a "bonus pick." In those days there was an arrangement whereby each club enjoyed one special pick before the regular draft started. It was Green Bay's turn after the 1956 season, and they went with Paul.

The pro draft was first set up in 1936 as a means of giving the have-nots a chance to catch up with the haves. Previously, the best talent had gone to the highest bidders. These were usually the clubs with the greatest amount of money to offer. And money meant having a crowd attraction—in other words, a winner.

It was a vicious cycle, but naturally a number of the more powerful clubs fought the draft. However, Bert Bell, president of the Philadelphia Eagles and a man who was later to become one of the most important commissioners in the game's history, proposed it and pushed it through.

At the time they weren't tearing down the gates at Shibe Park in Philadelphia to see Bert's clubs play. In fact, Bell used to say he could pick out all his friends in the stands. The Eagles drew a modest ten thousand for their better attractions while the University of Pennsylvania's high-powered college teams drew seventy thousand in Franklin Field. Bert, who died in 1959 watching the Eagles play, lived long enough to see the situation reversed in Philadelphia, the Eagles playing in Franklin Field and filling it every Sunday while his old alma mater attracted only a scattering of Ivy League followers on Saturday.

The 1956 draft has to be among the more famous in history, although I like to think that the draft after the 1954 season had a certain importance, too. That was the one in which Pittsburgh picked me on the ninth round.

Three of the first four men chosen in the 1956 draft were quarterbacks, Hornung to Green Bay, John Brodie to San Francisco, and Len Dawson to Purdue. Green Bay also took Ron Kramer, the end, from Michigan.

Cleveland took Jim Brown, looking for a breakaway runner but never dreaming how well they had picked. Still, Green Bay didn't do too badly with a quarterback who turned out to be about as versatile an offensive player as I've seen.

In 1960 Hornung racked up 671 yards rushing, caught a couple of touchdown passes, kicked fifteen field goals and forty-one extra points, and passed for a couple of TDs. It was an awesome performance, but I still think his five-touchdown game against us in 1965 was as impressive as anything he ever did on the field.

That's because the Hornung who played against us that

misty afternoon was virtually a shell of the great Hornung of the early sixties. He had been playing with a neck injury for a season or two, something which the Packers, understandably, soft-pedaled. But the old abandon was gone, and when Hornung scored thirty points against us that day he did it coming off the bench he had occupied for the two previous games.

We had lost one (to the Bears) and tied one (with Detroit) in our last two games. Against the Bears the previous week I had suffered a knee injury which put me on crutches for the rest of the year.

Hornung scored the game's first two touchdowns, one on a two-yard run, the other on a long pass from Bart Starr. We had two first-period field goals by Lou Michaels, one for forty-five yards, and then Lenny Moore got us a touchdown and we were only a point behind.

There wasn't too much time left in the second period when the Packers pulled off one of the biggest plays of the year. Gary Cuozzo was our quarterback and had been doing well. A recovered fumble had us down on their two, and it looked as though we'd go to the clubhouse with a lead.

Gary tried to fake Lenny Moore to the inside and Jerry Hill, our fullback, tried to sneak to the outside for a short pass. But Willie Davis, the Packer defensive end, had read the play and so had Dave Robinson, the Packer linebacker on that side. Davis almost intercepted. The ball got past his fingertips, but it didn't get past Robinson, who caught it, chest-high, and went eighty-eight yards with it to our ten. Starr had nineteen seconds to score and he made it with a comfortable margin. On the next play he completed a pass to Boyd Dowler in the back of the end zone.

In the third quarter Green Bay really opened up, thanks to Hornung. He got two more TDs, one on a nine-yarder, the other on a three. He ran as though someone had turned back the clock for him, and had rubbed away that gnawing ache in his neck.

Cuozzo hurt his shoulder in the third period and Don Shula, scarcely able to believe our bad luck, had to go to Tom Matte, who had last played quarterback when he was in college. We weren't to know until after the game that Gary had suffered a shoulder separation. He merely went into the clubhouse where the shoulder was taped and he was given a numbing injection of Novocain. He came back and got into the Packers with a series of good passes, taking us in for a couple of touchdowns that closed the gap to eight points with six minutes to play.

By this time the fog was so bad that fans in the upper deck were unable to see what was going on. The uproar was so great you couldn't hear. But Bart Starr ended our hopes when he threw the longest pass of the day to Hornung with 4½ minutes to play.

It was a third-and-nine situation. We blitzed and Hornung went up the middle, while Taylor stayed behind to pass-block for Starr. Starr hit Hornung about fifteen yards downfield and he went all the way. He was wide open because our middle linebacker had blitzed.

That was loss No. 2 to the Packers in 1965, a figure usually regarded as the maximum in any one season. However, there was the memorable Western Conference playoff to come two weeks later. I watched it on crutches from the sideline, Gary was back home in Baltimore recovering from shoulder surgery, and Tom Matte, who had earned his living in the pros by running with the ball, almost pulled off the football trick of the century in five desperate quarters of play in Green Bay. Altogether it was one of the weirdest seasons ever.

Paul Hornung, who scored almost twice as many touchdowns on that one afternoon in Baltimore as he did all through the 1965 season, would most certainly agree.

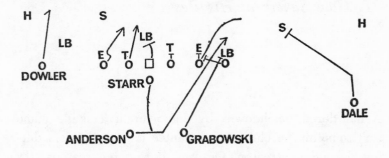

5. Typical Green Bay Power Play

The Packers' big play for vital short yardage or a scoring threat, used first with Hornung or Taylor and now with Grabowski or Anderson. Starr hands off to Anderson, who goes outside the opposing left end. The end is blocked and driven in; the other back takes the outside linebacker.

THE GAME: *Chicago vs. San Francisco*
THE PLACE: *Chicago*
THE TIME: *December 12, 1965*
FINAL SCORE: *Chicago, 61; San Francisco, 20*

21. Gale Sayers at His Best

A half-dozen touchdowns by one man in a single game isn't something a club can guarantee its ticketholders during the average season. Or even during ten seasons. It's happened only three times in the half-century the National Football League has been in existence. Oddly, the Chicago Bears have been involved each time, but only once on the winning end.

The first time it happened Ernie Nevers, of the Chicago Cardinals, ran for six TDs on Thanksgiving Day 1929. Twenty-two years later Cleveland's Dub Jones scored four TDs running and two passing. Then, fourteen years later, along came Gale Sayers to enjoy the greatest running year a rookie has ever had. On a bleak, raw afternoon in the Windy City, Sayers did it a little differently, putting together a pass, four assorted runs, and an eighty-five-yard punt return to total 336 yards. Only two performers have topped this aggregate yardage figure, Sayers himself the following year, and Timmy Brown, who came to the Colts from the Eagles in 1968.

Of the three men who had scored six touchdowns in a game, Sayers is the only one I've seen perform. Nevers, a Hall of Famer who played as many as thirty games a season with the Duluth Eskimos, finished up a couple of years before I was born. Dub Jones played for the Browns in both the All-America Conference and the National League; he was their big runner just about the time I was getting ready to enroll at St. Justin High School in Pittsburgh.

I've seen a good deal of Gale, however, and although I think Jimmy Brown was the best rusher of them all, I've never seen anyone with Sayers' ability to cut either way while going at full speed.

First let's talk about his speed. We watch films a great deal getting ready for the next week's game, and the game after that, and after that. But there isn't any real way to get ready for Sayers, and I'll tell you why. It was either in his first or second season, and the Bears were coming up. We got the films and ran them through. On one particular play Don Shula said, "Wait a minute, what was that?"

It was a kickoff runback by Sayers, only there wasn't much we could see of him. When he caught the ball he took off so fast that he was actually just a blur on the film. There wasn't any imperfection in the film because everyone else was nice and clear. All you could see of Sayers were some blurry lines.

Sayers isn't very big—six feet and two hundred pounds—and you'd expect that a runner of these dimensions would keep pretty well to the outside. But he can hit inside as well as anyone in the game today, which makes him a deadly threat. He can even bull his way across for a yard against a stacked defense as he did for one of his half-dozen touchdowns against San Francisco on his biggest day.

Rudy Bukich was the Bears' quarterback, and he started the party with a screen pass to Sayers in the opening period. Sayers simply took off and went eighty yards for the first TD. In the second period Gale scored on runs of twenty-one and seven yards. In the third he cut through tackle and went fifty yards. Later in the period Gale slammed through from the one. Then in the final period the 49ers made the mistake of putting a punt within Gale's catching range. He returned it eighty-five yards, all the way.

The Chicago Bears have never lacked superior runners. In fact, the only rookie ever to rush for a thousand yards in one season was the Bears' Beattie Feathers back in 1934. In the thirties Bronko Nagurski, a smashing fullback who left a wake of broken limbs, was a Bears' superstar. In the mid-fifties Rick Casares came along to gain thousand-yard stature.

The Bears won the title in 1963 without any first-class runner, and the Chicago management began to feel a pressing need for one after the club had slipped from its championship peak. Sayers was a great college performer at Kansas, and the Bears became involved in a bidding match with the Kansas City Chiefs for his services.

Sayers and his linebacking teammate from Illinois, Dick Butkus, who has proved to be an outstanding defensive player in the pros, represented two of the heaviest investments in the Bears' history.

But there is no question that getting Sayers was one of the smartest talent moves George Halas has made in his Bears a performer able to register a record twenty-two TDs half-century in pro ball. His investment in Sayers gave the in one season. For the foreseeable future, all Bears' championship bids, of necessity, must be built around Sayers' agility and speed.

22. Jackie Does It Again

About the only greater satisfaction a traded quarterback can get beyond beating the team that traded him in a title game is doing it via a shutout. Jackie Kemp enjoyed that sensation in the American League's 1965 title game when Buffalo beat San Diego, 23–0. The victory came exactly one year after the Bills had beaten this same team 20–7, but the 1965 game represented a peak for the Bills on several counts.

For one thing even Buffalo's presence in the title game was a little unusual. Kemp was without his two big receivers, Elbert Dubenion and Glenn Bass, during most of the season. In 1964 they accounted for a total of seventeen touchdowns. In 1965 they each caught one before being sidelined with leg injuries. Their loss forced Lou Saban to adopt a rare double tight end offense. Fortunately Lou had the personnel for this in Ernie Warlick and Paul Costa. Both were comparatively fast for their identical six-four, 235-pound measurements.

Then, too, Buffalo was operating without Cookie Gilchrist, who had been traded after the championship 1964 campaign. Cookie had led the league in rushing two out of three years, and had accounted for 122 yards rushing against the Chargers. He went to Denver for Billy Joe, another large fullback who complained of bunions.

But although Buffalo was not as impressive as it was the previous year, when it won all but two of its games, it didn't have to be. The Eastern Division failed to produce another team able to top the .500 level, which put the Bills back in the playoff. Only this time it was in sunny Southern California instead of cold, damp Buffalo.

Kemp knew the area well. A native Californian, he bounced around a bit after he was drafted seventeenth by the Lions in 1957 when he graduated from Occidental. The Lions thought they were set with quarterbacks and dealt him to Pittsburgh for a couple of lower draft choices, obviously a good deal for Detroit.

Pittsburgh gave him a brief look (which is more than they gave me), and the record shows he threw a total of eighteen passes for the Steelers, completing eight. They released him and he was on the Giants' taxi squad in 1958, and the 49ers' taxi squad in 1959. He also put in some time with the Calgary club. He had just about come to the end of the line when Lamar Hunt and Harry Wismer got together a lot of their millionaire friends for a try at a second major league.

Sid Gillman, who was picked to run the Los Angeles club in the new league, was aware of Kemp's abilities and signed him as a free agent. He had a playoff quarterback for the next two seasons.

In the third year Jackie sustained an injury to the middle finger of his passing hand. Every time the center handed the ball back to him with the necessary smack, the finger went out of joint. Jackie was able to pass with it all right, but everyone could see him yanking it back into place on his way to the huddle.

This must have made Sid Gillman nervous because the

next thing, there was the league's leading passer one year removed, up on one-hundred-dollar waivers. Buffalo, struggling along with ordinary personnel at quarterback, figured it had nothing to lose except the price of the message to league headquarters. To the Bills' vast surprise the waivers were not withdrawn and Kemp had a new employer. Subsequently, Gillman had a hard time explaining how he let a first-class quarterback go for a hundred dollars. After a year or two the Chargers simply stopped trying to explain. Kemp's appearance in the 1962 all-star game, the year he was traded, didn't help with the Charger fans, either.

San Diego never had a chance in the 1965 title game. The Chargers were unable to penetrate beyond the Bills' twenty-four-yard line. In the second period Kemp threw a scoring pass to Warlick. Before the half ended Butch Byrd, a Bills' cornerback, had returned a punt for seventy-four yards and Buffalo was in front, 14–0.

During the second half the Bills' kicker, Pete Gogolak, went to work. Gogolak had been a soccer-type kicker with the Cornell University team. His style was an immediate success with Buffalo, and in the 1965 game he booted three to make the rout of the Chargers complete.

The Chargers had placed heavy reliance on the passing combination of John Hadl and Lance Alworth. This pair had accounted for fourteen touchdowns during the regular season. Buffalo met the challenge by double-teaming Alworth to the point where he became discouraged. The maneuver left one receiver open, but there was little he could do with the Bills' defense putting on a massive rush that all but smothered Hadl. Hadl thought he had a threat going in the second half when San Diego gained a fourth-and-one on the twenty-nine. But then there was a blown handoff and that threat, too, dissipated.

The oddest aspect of the AFL season was still to come. The following week Lou Saban dropped a bombshell. He was leaving his head-coach job with the Bills to return to college football at the University of Maryland. Saban declared that big bonuses had spoiled the pro game.

"I'm tired of dealing with lawyers and accountants who don't know a damned thing about football instead of talking with the boy and trying to sell him on our club. There's no more fun in the game."

Saban, in turn, had a surprise due him. Six months later the two leagues got together and the crazy bidding stopped. Apparently that put the fun back into it for Lou, because he left Maryland after a year and took over as head coach and general manager of the Denver club.

THE GAME: *Baltimore vs. Green Bay*
THE PLACE: *Green Bay*
THE TIME: *December 26, 1965*
FINAL SCORE: *Green Bay, 13; Baltimore, 10*

23. 1965—A Year to Remember

After the 1964 season, I sat down with my longtime friend, Ed Fitzgerald, assembled a lot of scattered thoughts, and committed them to paper. The book that resulted was titled, *Pro Quarterback: My Own Story.* Those who insist that this life-story effort was a little premature certainly have a strong argument, for 1965 turned out to be the most dramatic year in my career.

If you check the *Football Register* you'll discover it was the first season since 1958 in which I didn't appear in every game the Colts played. And for an excellent reason —midseason surgery.

To start at the beginning, we were coming off a Western Conference championship season in which we had beaten the Packers twice before losing to Cleveland in the 1964 playoff. Green Bay got its revenge in 1965, beating us either twice or three times, depending on your point of view.

First they beat us in the second game of the year in Green Bay, scoring the three points that made the difference in the last few minutes. Then we won five in a row, coming up to our first game with the Bears. We won the game in Chicago, although it was close, but I came out

of it with a bad back. Gary Cuozzo finished up, and the
following week, in Minnesota, Gary threw five TD passes,
which is still the Colts' individual record. I had a lot of
passing records, but I've never thrown five touchdown
passes in a game.

I returned the following week and played in a 24–24 tie
with the Lions, and there went our winning streak. It was
also to prove the beginning of our troubles.

We were back home the next week before a friendly
crowd of more than sixty thousand fans playing the un-
friendly Bears again. This was the game in which I suffered
the most serious injury of my career. It happened late in
the second period. Attempting to pass to John Mackey,
our tight end, I tore the ligaments in my right knee. I
finished the rest of the year on crutches.

From the movies I've been able to reconstruct what
happened. I had gotten the ball off, but one of their
defensive linemen, Stan Jones, had a pretty good grip on
my leg as I unloaded. Another lineman, Ted Karras, came
charging in and apparently was unable to hold back. I
was bent over backward and the way he hit me simply
put an unbearable stress on the cartilage. It snapped as I
toppled over.

It's funny how things go in football. You drive to a ball
game in midmorning with everything blotted from your
mind but the day's game plan. Twenty-four hours later
you're thinking completely different thoughts because you
have been under the surgeon's scalpel and your leg is in a
cast from your hip down.

A professional player thinks football no matter what
other stress he's under, so I couldn't help but consider
just a little bitterly that had we beaten the Bears we
would have wrapped up the Western title for a second
straight year. Instead, we now had a mere half-game lead

on Green Bay and they were coming to town the following week.

Elsewhere I've described how they won that game with one of the greatest performances in Paul Hornung's career. The shoulder separation Gary Cuozzo sustained that afternoon put him out of action for the rest of the year, and if any other contending club anywhere in pro history has lost two quarterbacks on successive weeks it's a record which has escaped me.

Losing to the Packers dropped us behind them in the conference standings. The following week we beat the Rams, using Tom Matte, a running back, and Ed Brown, a Steelers pickup, at quarterback. Meanwhile Green Bay was held to a 24–24 tie by a San Francisco club that barely topped .500 for the season.

So that brought us face to face with the Packers for a third time, in Green Bay. We spent Christmas in that Arctic outpost, not straying too far from our hotel headquarters. Baltimore gets chilly occasionally and western Pennsylvania, where I grew up, has had its cold snaps, but for the real vein-congealing cold you have to tip your hat to Green Bay. The 1967 championship game was played there in thirteen below weather with a good stiff wind blowing. Did you know that schoolchildren in Green Bay are disappointed when they get up in the morning and the thermometer registers only twenty below? That's because school is never called off unless the temperature dips to twenty-five below or worse.

Well, we sank out of the 1965 race after almost fourteen minutes of a record overtime period. The game was won when Don Chandler, the Green Bay place kicker, booted his second successful field goal in three tries during that long, cold afternoon. We have always maintained that Chandler actually made only one of these three. The movies of the game prove it, too, but no decision in pro football has ever been reversed on what showed up the next day, or the day after that, on the silver screen, and maybe that's the way it should be.

But I'd like to say a word about those movies, particularly the part that showed Chandler's twenty-two-yard game-tying field goal in the final moments of the fourth quarter. The following spring I was one of a group of football players who toured Army posts in Vietnam. The National League office provided us with a number of game films. Included, without our having asked for it, was the 1965 Western Conference playoff. The camera was positioned right behind the goal posts on the field-goal attempt, and it clearly showed the ball going wide.

Don't take my word for it, ask the hundreds of soldiers who saw the film. You could hear them yell a block away when the official raised his arms signaling that the kick was good.

Willie Davis, the Green Bay defensive end, was on that trip, along with Sam Huff and Frank Gifford. Willie came in for a lot of ribbing about the quality of the field goal, but he always had a standard response, delivered with a grin.

"I don't know whether it was good or not," Willie would say, "but I have a seven-thousand-dollar check back home that says it was." Willie was having his little joke. Among other things, the winning playoff check had long since been cashed.

Let me give you a tip on field goals. This comes from Pat Summerall, who was a pretty good place-kicker himself before he moved into the radio-TV field. Says Summerall: "Don't watch the ball, watch the kicker. By the way he acts you'll know whether the kick was good or not."

From the way Chandler acted you'd have thought a

twister had lifted the roof off his house in Oklahoma. He changed pretty fast, though, when he got a look at the official with his arms up in the air.

Green Bay played with a sub quarterback after Bart Starr was hurt early in the first half. He was attempting to tackle Don Shinnick, one of our linebackers, who had recovered a fumble and went on to score. After that Zeke Bratkowski directed the club, and Starr just held the ball for the place kicks. Even so, the Packers outpassed us 250 net yards to 32.

The remainder of the season was an anticlimax; at least it was for us. The Packers beat the Browns for the NFL title the following Sunday on the same field. We had a week's rest and then went down to Miami to play Dallas, runners-up in the East, in the Playoff Bowl. We won that one 35–3, and Tom Matte threw a couple of touchdown passes. Fortunately, it hasn't been necessary for him to do any passing since.

There was one other Baltimore injury that memorable year, and although no injury can ever really be described as "funny," this one, to Jimmy Orr, the receiver, had overtones of humor. It happened when we were playing the Eagles, just before I was hurt in the Chicago game. On one particular drive we were moving the ball pretty well when Jimmy injured his shoulder.

It didn't look too good, so they took him over to Union Memorial Hospital, which is only a few blocks from the Baltimore ball park, to be X-rayed. We figured we had seen the last of him for a while at least, but darned if three drives later Jimmy wasn't back!

The X-rays had shown that there wasn't any break. He grabbed a cab back to the field and arrived while we had possession. When he ran out on the field whoever we had in there in his place naturally ran off.

I didn't know it at the time but Don Shula, our coach, had sent Jimmy in primarily as a receiver decoy. Two plays later he went deep for a pass, caught it, and scored a touchdown. I often wonder how Jimmy paid the cab driver that day because he had his uniform on and football uniforms don't have pockets for change.

THE GAME: *Dallas vs. Green Bay*
THE PLACE: *Dallas*
THE TIME: *January 1, 1967*
FINAL SCORE: *Green Bay, 34; Dallas, 27*

24. Big Doings in Dallas

Dallas's comparatively brief history in pro football has seldom lacked for suspense and excitement. A decade and a half ago the state was unable to support a pro team. From that point Lone Star football has developed into a bitter clash between rival leagues, capped by successive-year Dallas Cowboy bids for the NFL championship.

Newspapermen going to the Cotton Bowl for pro football only a few years ago would joke, "Bring a bow and arrow with you, you'll be able to shoot a deer in the upper stands."

Today the Cowboys have, with rare exception, taken the play away from southwestern college football, which has always been highly popular. Not that the quality of college football has declined; it's just that the Cowboys have come up with a winning ball club.

Pro ball was first introduced into the area in the early fifties. A sportsmen's group, several years ahead of its time, obtained the franchise of the New York Yankees, named it the Dallas Texans, and then sat back to wait for the customers. There weren't any.

After a couple of utter disasters at the gate, they threw in the underfinanced sponge and the league took the operation over. The Texans finished the season as a "road club," meaning it played in a different city each week until the lamentable experiment ended.

The Texans had such players as Buddy Young, Artie Donovan, George Ratterman, and John Rauch, who was later to serve as a head coach with Oakland in the Super Bowl. The talent was certainly there. They were merely in town a decade too early.

The Texans won one of a dozen games, then quietly disappeared, their playing days apparently at an end. Here Bert Bell's genius for selling pro football entered the picture. The NFL commissioner convinced Carroll Rosenbloom, a close friend, that Baltimore, which had had two previous nonprofit shots, one in the All-America Conference, the other for a year in the NFL after the merger, offered a superb opportunity. Rosenbloom, who had known Bell from back in his University of Pennsylvania days, went for the pitch. The rest is history.

Dallas, meanwhile, was without a pro team until the sixties when the NFL, seeking to head off the American League in that area, issued a franchise to Clint Murchison, Jr. He had the right kind of money to stick with it for a while. So did Lamar Hunt, one of the organizers of the rival league. Both clubs played in the Cotton Bowl, a civic property. Both took enormous baths in red ink. Hunt's Texans were the first to quit.

Hunt stayed in Dallas for three years, then moved a winning ball club to Kansas City. The Cowboys, he said, could have the territory to themselves, and good riddance.

But at about the same time Tom Landry's meticulous brand of coaching began to take hold. The Cowboys placed fourth in 1964 and second in 1965. In 1966 the first title game was played in the Cotton Bowl, which had suddenly become a magnet for every pro football fan in the Southwest.

Dallas stacked up well against Green Bay. The Packers had been one of the Cowboys' five successive preseason victims in 1966. And over the regular-season fourteen-game schedule they had outscored the Packers by more than one hundred points. Undoubtedly there was a lot of respect for the Packers in the Cowboy camp, but there was no reason for Dallas to lack confidence. Not when they had linemen just as big and receivers just as fast.

More than seventy-five thousand fans were treated to the first decent playoff weather in a half-dozen years, weather in which the participants didn't have to worry about whether their fingers would freeze around the ball.

Within the first five minutes, it looked as though the Cowboys might have been just a little too cocky. The Packers culminated a seventy-six-yard drive with a Bart Starr pass to Elijah Pitts, and less than a quarter of a minute later Green Bay made it 14–0 with a fumble return by Jim Grabowski.

But as it turned out, the Cowboys hadn't even gotten their spurs adjusted. When they did, they engineered a pair of TD drives that tied the score just as the quarter ended. Dan Reeves went over from the three on the first march, and then Don Perkins scored on a twenty-three-yard run.

In the second period the Packers moved ahead when Starr connected with Carroll Dale, and they stayed in front despite a field goal by Danny Villanueva, which brought the Cowboys to within 21–17 at the half.

Villanueva got another in the third period to bring the Cowboys to within a point, but a Starr pass to Boyd Dowler put some daylight between them, and one to Max McGee, with two-thirds of the final period gone, apparently put the game beyond the Cowboys' grasp. It seemed of small importance that Don Chandler, who had kicked all three extra points, had his final one blocked by Bob Lilly.

But Meredith got off a sixty-eight-yard bomb to the Dallas tight end, Frank Clarke, a minute later and suddenly it was a ball game again. Another Dallas TD would tie things up. That missed extra point began to loom bigger and bigger.

Two minutes remained when Meredith hit Frank Clarke with a twenty-one-yard pass. Perkins then went up the middle for four. Meredith failed on another pass to Clarke, this one with the receiver in the end zone. The Dallas fans groaned, but the umpire signaled a pass interference call against Tom Brown, the Green Bay safety.

In a deafening din the Cowboys moved up to the two with a minute and fifty-two seconds left to make the touchdown that would send the game into overtime. On the first play Dan Reeves picked up a yard off right tackle. Meredith had his strategy all laid out. The off-tackle play was to be followed by a quarterback rollout and then two wedges to get in. A "wedge" is just what the term implies, a running play from up close in which the runner tries to ram into the end zone behind a wall of blockers.

Meredith proceeded to roll out and threw to Pettis Norman in the end zone. Norman dropped the ball. There was an offside call on the play, so instead of resuming at the one-yard line again, the Cowboys found themselves back at the six.

This changed Meredith's strategy. He faked Perkins into the line and threw a pass to Reeves in the flat. Reeves dropped it. The enormous pressures on the Cowboys were having their effect.

Meredith passed again. Norman and Buddy Dial, the flanker, were running a crossing pattern and Norman had broken loose at the sideline. The pass proved just a little low. Norman managed to catch it on the two but was stopped right there.

Tom Landry vividly recalls the next play, the play that decided the NFL title. So do most of the forty million fans who watched on TV. Meredith rolled out to the right with the option of running or passing to Bob Hayes, the split end. He was to take his cue from what the Packers did.

The idea was to isolate the cornerback covering Hayes. If he stayed with Hayes, Meredith was to run the ball in. If he came up, Meredith would pass to Hayes. The guard was to pull out to take the linebacker on that side.

The Cowboys had scored many times on that play, but they weren't counting on a great effort by Dave Robinson. The Green Bay outside linebacker gambled by overplaying in his efforts to delay Hayes. Then Robinson came through on the inside so fast he went right by the guard, who couldn't pick him up. The "correct" procedure would have been for Dave to come in front of the guard and cause Meredith to hold up, leaving Hayes to the safetyman.

Robinson grabbed Meredith by the left arm and pulled, just as the Dallas quarterback got off a desperation pass in the direction of the end zone, using a sort of underhand motion.

Tom Brown was waiting, the same Brown who had been charged with pass interference minutes earlier. He was supposed to be covering Reeves on the play but had lost him. "I saw Hayes on the left and Clarke on the right," explained Brown. "I was between them and just right there when the ball came down."

Starr then held the ball on two running plays to consume the remaining half-minute. It was one of the most dramatic of playoff finishes. The exhausted players were convinced that they would never again be involved in such last-ditch heroics, with so much at stake (the victory, along with a possible subsequent victory in the first Super Bowl two weeks later, was worth in the vicinity of twenty-three thousand dollars per player).

They were wrong. Twelve months later the same two clubs were to meet again in a battle for the NFL title.

THE GAME: *Green Bay vs. Kansas City*
THE PLACE: *Los Angeles*
THE TIME: *January 15, 1967*
FINAL SCORE: *Green Bay, 35; Kansas City, 10*

25. That First Time

January is a month when football players usually catch up on the household chores, get a little indigestion at various banquets, and try to rest. January 1967, by contrast, was one of the busiest months I've ever had. I put in a lot of mileage and played in two Bowls, the Playoff Bowl in Miami and the Pro Bowl in Los Angeles.

The one Bowl I really wanted to get into, however, the Super, had a "no admission" sign. The Green Bay Packers, who won three more games during the 1966 season than we did, had hung it there.

There'll be a great many Super Bowls, or whatever they'll wind up calling the big game between the National and American Leagues, but there was only one first Super Bowl.

It's always nice to be a part of history, and the game between the Packers and the Kansas City Chiefs will be history for a great many reasons, not the least of which is that it will probably stand as the only Super Bowl in which there were thirty thousand empty seats.

The next year the Packers and the Oakland Raiders packed the Orange Bowl in Miami with the same attraction. Some observers claim that the reason the first Super Bowl was such a difficult event to sell was that Californians couldn't care less about a local sports attraction unless one of their own teams is involved.

Others say it was impossible to sell Green Bay vs. Kansas City as any kind of a matchup, and the second half of that game gave a lot of weight to this argument. Anyway, it would be interesting to take the Super Bowl back to the Los Angeles Coliseum a half-dozen years from now and see how it draws. With the Rams playing you could take it back tomorrow and be assured of a sellout.

The fans at the first Super Bowl weren't aware that both Jim Taylor and Paul Hornung were playing their last game as Packers.

Hornung watched from the sideline. Later, Vince Lombardi said he would have used him only if the Packers had needed an inspirational lift. Considering the seriousness of Hornung's neck injury it's probable that Vince was only saying something nice about a once-great competitor. Hornung, of course, later went to New Orleans in the expansion draft and retired.

Taylor picked up fifty-three yards and one touchdown in his Super Bowl effort. It was all that proved necessary because Bart Starr was able to solve the Kansas City defense in a hurry and pick it apart. He threw a couple of touchdown passes, and in the second half the Chiefs never penetrated deeper than five yards into Green Bay territory. At the end there were twenty-five points separating the two clubs.

The play that probably took the most out of Kansas City was one of Starr's favorites, that third-and-short-yardage where he fakes his fullback into the line, then uncorks a long pass to one of his wide receivers. It came in the second quarter with the score tied and the Packers on the Kansas City thirty-six.

Taylor faked into the line and this brought Fred Williamson, one of the Kansas City cornerbacks, up too hard. Carroll Dale went by him in a hurry and took a long pass in the clear for a touchdown.

There was a penalty on the play and it was called back, but Green Bay's superiority was clearly established at this point. Taylor scored later in the same period on one of Green Bay's classic power plays, a sweep to the left in which the tackle hooks the end and the two guards (Jerry Kramer and Fuzzy Thurston) mop up. That made it 14–7, and the best Kansas City could do before the half ended was a thirty-one-yard field goal by Mike Mercer.

When the Packers opened their bag of blitzing tricks after the intermission, it marked the end of the Chiefs. Dave Robinson, the outside linebacker, looped in and tipped one of Lenny Dawson's passes. Willie Wood picked it off and went from midfield down to the five where Mike Garrett stopped him from behind. That tackle was probably Kansas City's best defensive effort of the game. Elijah Pitts scored on the next play.

After that the Packers wore down the Chiefs steadily, and one of the highpoints was the manner in which Starr continued to connect with veteran Max McGee, who was standing in at flanker for the injured Boyd Dowler. McGee had scored the first TD when he beat Willie Mitchell on an inside move, reaching back with one hand to snap the ball to his chest. This had been balanced by one of Lenny Dawson's passes out of the floating pocket to Curtis Mc-Clinton, the big Kansas City fullback, but it was to be the Chiefs' only touchdown all afternoon.

McGee, who was originally set to watch the game from a comfortable seat on the sideline, caught seven passes, almost twice as many as anyone else caught in the game and almost twice as many as Max had caught all season.

McGee always did have a good sense of timing, and he

announced his retirement immediately after the game. When questioned about it Vince Lombardi issued one of his patented grins and remarked, "He hasn't told *me* yet."

It turned out Max hadn't, either. When the 1967 season opened, there was McGee at the Packers' training camp at St. Norbert's in West DePere. He caught three passes all through the regular 1967 season, then grabbed one for thirty-five yards in Super Bowl No. 2 against Oakland.

Then Max really retired.

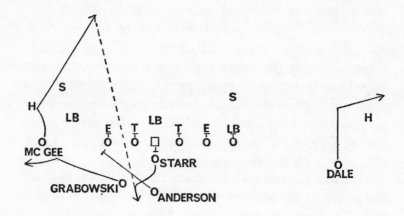

6. Green Bay Play-Action Pass (Starr to McGee)

One of Green Bay's favorite plays, used in third-down, short-yardage situations. Starr is outstanding in disguising his intent until the final split second.

THE GAME: *New York vs. San Diego*
THE PLACE: *San Diego*
THE TIME: *December 24, 1967*
FINAL SCORE: *New York, 42; San Diego, 31*

26. Joe Namath Tops the Four-Thousand Mark

When I first came into pro ball, two thousand yards' worth of passing in a twelve-game season was a rather respectable figure. The big target was three thousand yards. Sammy Baugh had come closest, with 2938 for the 1947 Redskins. My first year, 1956, Tobin Rote had 2203 for Green Bay, and that was the highest in the league.

Even without counting the two extra games that were added to the schedule in the early sixties, times have obviously changed. A half-dozen men in the National League topped three thousand yards in 1967; half that many did it in the American League. In addition, Joe Namath, of the New York Jets, became the first to break through the four-thousand-yard mark, during that season. It makes you wonder who will be the first passer to hit five thousand in one year.

From a promotional and public relations point of view, Namath is the most important performer to come into the American Football League. No major sports operation has ever enjoyed financial success without a strong New York anchor. There are a good number of reasons, ranging from the fact that, like it or not, New York is the communications center of the country, to the desire of fans in other locations to root *against* someone.

Take the case of the New York Yankees, for instance. For years they yelled "break up the Yankees," meaning "give someone else a chance," and when the Yankees dropped into the second division everyone was happy—for a very brief while.

Then the awful truth dawned. The Yankees as a visiting attraction were worth twice as much as any other club —when they were on top. When the second-division Yankees showed up, the fans didn't.

After taking over as commissioner, Pete Rozelle promptly moved the NFL's headquarters from Philadelphia to New York. It had been in Philadelphia because Bert Bell came from there. Pete was a Californian and he knew that no one would hold still for taking the headquarters to California, so he picked the best possible spot.

The American League, in deference to the oil and cattle money backing it, originally established its office in Dallas. They smartened up in a hurry and went to New York after a couple of years. In June of 1968 the two leagues moved under one Park Avenue roof.

Most of the other big-time sports have done the same. Baseball (which has given way to pro football as the nation's No. 1 sport according to a nationwide poll of the Associated Press's managing editors taken in the summer of 1967) has its commissioner positioned in New York. But it clings to the trolley-car idea that the presidents of the respective leagues can dictate the location of their headquarters. So for fifteen years the National League has been isolated in Cincinnati, where Warren Giles was once boss of the Cincinnati Reds, and the American League in Boston, where Joe Cronin was once general manager of the Red Sox.

The most charitable thing that can be said about this setup is that baseball doesn't like change.

When Sonny Werblin rounded up four of his friends to put in with him in equal shares to buy the bankrupt New York Titans, he was well aware of the chance he was taking. Werblin and his friends knew they would have to play at least one year in a rat's nest called the Polo Grounds while the city fiddled around taking an extra year to build Shea Stadium across from the New York World's Fair. He knew, too, that he had to gamble on the best talent available, but he realized that if he didn't make it there wasn't much chance for the league, either. The other teams had been coming in to play to crowds of two thousand or three thousand in New York, which was a disaster.

The Jets invested heavily in talent, and as the saying goes, they won some and they lost some. Remember John Huarte and Cosmo Iacavazzi and Bob Schweikert? Those were some of the six-figure bonus rookies who never panned out. However, the Jets' bookkeeping department took its licking without a whimper. Easing the pain was Joe Willie Namath of Beaver Falls, Pennsylvania.

The amount of tape and bandage used to wrap Namath's two bad legs could just about balance the amount of newsprint describing his various ailments. Reams have been written about what would happen to the Jets if Joe Namath failed to get up after a particular play.

He's a tough young man, though, and he's taken the best shots thrown at him. He keeps coming, and for this the entire American League can be grateful.

I've followed Namath's career more than most of the other AFL quarterbacks because he's from the same western Pennsylvania area as I am. I've always been very grateful to my alma mater, the University of Louisville, for the many good things it did for me during my college career. My old coach, Frank Camp, and his assistants helped me get started in the pros. So when my efforts to get Namath to attend Louisville didn't work out I was disappointed.

As everyone knows, he went to Alabama where he became one of the country's top college stars in the early sixties. Then the Jets easily outbid the Cardinals, the NFL team which drafted him, and he went to New York where my first Colt coach, Weeb Ewbank, got him.

Namath made rookie-of-the-year in his first campaign and was always one of the league's first three or four passers in his first few years. The pros rate passers on a formula where equal credit is given for completion percentage, touchdown passes, interception percentage, and average gain. It is a pretty accurate gauge.

In 1967 it appeared that Joe was going to be the passer to lead the Jets to their first divisional title. They were way out in front at midseason, but they slipped badly at the end. They had to sit by and watch the Houston club beat Miami on TV for the Eastern title while they waited to wrap up the season the next day in San Diego in a game which had no further meaning in the race.

Namath, however, put some sort of meaning into that final game from a passing-record viewpoint. He had been injured the previous week in collisions with two of Oakland's larger pass rushers, Ike Lassiter and Ben Davidson, and he wore a special mask to protect a broken cheekbone. Despite this handicap he threw one touchdown pass to George Sauer and three to Don Maynard. This pair finished one-two among the pass receivers in the AFL that season, which is quite a feat.

In the National League, Sonny Jurgensen, of the Washington Redskins, had broken his own record in passing yardage a week earlier. When Jurgy was with the 1961

Eagles he had thrown for 3723 yards. With Washington in 1967 he added twenty-four more yards.

Namath didn't fool around with short gains. He was good for 343 yards into the fourth quarter (when the Jets dropped away from the passing game to protect their lead), and he wound up with 4007.

As I've always maintained, football is no game for anyone who worries too much about a few aches and pains. I missed two games in 1958 with some broken ribs and a punctured lung. Sure it hurt when I got back but the doctors, who should know more about these things than football players, told me I could play. So I did, and I was in the championship playoff that year. There have been a number of other bumps and bruises since, and you have to expect them as long as you stay in the game.

It's probably the same with Namath. He wears a special brace for his bad knee and it looks like a piece of exhaust pipe you'd find alongside the highway after a pretty good auto wreck. They tell me he is wrapped from his hips to his toes when he plays, both legs. But the point is he plays and he's the best the Jets have had.

He has meant more to New York and the rest of the American League than any other player since the league started in 1960.

THE GAME: *Oakland vs. Houston*
THE PLACE: *Oakland*
THE TIME: *December 31, 1967*
FINAL SCORE: *Oakland, 40; Houston, 7*

27. *George Blanda's Comeback*

Sometimes when football coaches find it a little difficult
to fall asleep they'll have a kind of wakeful nightmare.
They'll think of all the players in the history of pro football
who have been traded away, only to come back and beat
their old clubs when it counted most.

The fact that he had better men at the time he made
the trade, that he was going with younger players, or that
the player he sent away had lost a step or a shade of his
accuracy, is small consolation for a coach as he watches
the dream-points go up on the scoreboard.

Such a situation existed on the last day of 1967 when
Oakland won its first American Football League crown
before a capacity crowd of 53,330 in its shiny new stadium.
George Blanda's four field goals, none shorter than thirty-
six yards, didn't exactly beat Houston, the club that had
let him go on waivers the previous September (Oakland's
ultimate edge was 40–7). But as a final indignity, Blanda
was used in relief at quarterback in the final six minutes
of a game long-since won.

The Oakland Raiders of 1967 were probably the best
team developed in the young league up to that point, a

direct tribute to the coaching ability and trading skill of
Al Davis, whose career in pro ball is a story in itself. Al
was the man who literally saved the Raiders' franchise
with a 10-4 coaching record in 1963 after they had lost
nineteen in a row under a string of previous coaches. The
AFL, in a desperate struggle for talent with our league,
then tapped him for a commissioner's role in 1966, only a
few months before peace was made between the two
leagues.

The reports were that Al received a sizable amount in the
AFL's settlement of his long-term contract, but even a fat
bank account isn't everything to a youngish man who has
been hired for a fighting commissioner's role, only to have
someone else call off the fight.

That would have chased most others into a different
field of endeavor, but not Al Davis. He went back to Oakland and convinced the two owners that they needed a
"managing partner." Under the direction of the new "managing partner" and head coach, John Rauch, the Raiders
had a comparatively modest 8-5-1 record in 1966. But in
1967, bolstered by a number of trades, the team breezed
to a Western Division title with a 13-1 record, losing only
to the New York Jets.

The trades included Hewritt Dixon, a 220-pounder from
Denver whom Davis converted from a tight end to a
fullback, and Daryle Lamonica, a twenty-five-year-old quarterback who had served an apprenticeship at Buffalo behind Jack Kemp.

To get Lamonica, Davis took a deep breath and a long
chance. He sent the Bills his quarterback, Tom Flores, and
Art Powell, a wide receiver, who has caught more TD
passes than anyone else in AFL history. Had this trade
backfired the customers might easily have pointed Davis

in the direction of the Bay Bridge. Instead, Lamonica threw thirty TD passes in the regular season, then two more in the playoff, and made Player of the Year in the league.

Dixon came in handy when Clem Daniels, the best rusher in Oakland history, fractured a foot in midseason against Miami. That finished him and projected Dixon to the front of the picture. In the playoff Dixon accounted for 144 yards rushing.

The 1967 playoff was a prime example of what can be done in pro football by trading for other clubs' unwanted personnel. For instance, both of Lamonica's TD passes were caught by men who had come to Oakland in trades. Dave Kocourek, who grabbed a looper for sixteen yards after a fake field goal just before halftime, had come from the Miami club; Bill Miller, the other TD receiver, was a Buffalo castoff (two weeks later he was to catch a couple of payoff passes against Green Bay in the Super Bowl).

But Blanda was the big story. He goes back to the late forties with the Chicago Bears where a wealth of quarter-backing with fellows like Sid Luckman and Johnny Lujack forced George Halas to turn Blanda into a linebacker. Blanda played in the 1956 championship against the Giants, and in 1958 decided he had had enough.

However, when the new league came along George went with the Houston Oilers, and he both ran the show and did the kicking on the clubs which won the 1960 and 1961 titles. Then Houston began looking for younger talent. They brought in Don Trull and later Pete Beathard, who came from Kansas City, and Blanda was rated expendable. His twelve points on a quartet of field goals (a league playoff record) in the 1967 title game and his personal high of 116 points for the season, which won him top honors in that department, indicate that the move may have been a little hasty.

Houston won the Eastern Division title despite having changed quarterbacks in midseason. A strong running attack, highlighted by Hoyle Granger's thousand-yard-plus effort, was the main reason Houston bounced back from a 3-11 year in 1966. For a number of seasons the Oilers had been looking for a runner to replace the hydrant-shaped Charlie Tolar, who was listed at a charitable five-six and 195 pounds on the rosters. They found their man in Granger (pronounced Gran-jair), a 225-pounder from Mississippi State. Oddly, both our club and the Oilers had picked Granger as a fifth choice in the last noncommon draft.

Unlike Oakland, which wrapped things up early (via a victory over the Oilers with two games to go), the Oilers had to win their divisional crown in the last game. That particular Oakland-Houston meeting in Houston was notable in that Blanda, giving his ex-home fans a treat, booted three second-half field goals to spoil Houston's 7–0 half-time lead.

Granger was actually second to Jim Nance, of Boston, in rushing for the year, but Oakland's reports rated Granger more dangerous. They gave him a higher mark on his ability to move laterally, and rated him a better receiver. "If we can shut him off," said Davis, "we can shut off Houston."

Houston counted heavily on Granger and its lesser ball-carriers. Said Wally Lemm, the Houston coach who had the distinction of coaching the Oilers early in their history, switching to the St. Louis Cardinals in the NFL, and returning for the 1966 season to Houston, "If you have the ball the other team can't score."

In the playoff, Granger had the ball for fourteen carries

and was stifled for a mere nineteen yards. The Raiders ran up a 30–0 lead until Beathard's five-yard touchdown pass to Charlie Frazier in the fourth period. Not once did they fumble, not once were any of Lamonica's two dozen pass attempts intercepted.

The Raiders pounded away at Houston's vulnerable right side. Oakland's front four of Tom Keating, Ben Davidson, Dan Birdwell, and Ike Lassiter pressured Beathard heavily. At the end, even the most ardent of customers were satisfied with Oakland's impressive victory.

The fans could be pardoned for a little excessive enthusiasm because Oakland's road had been long, tough, and winding. The club was almost an afterthought. When the AFL was shut out of Minneapolis the year it organized, the franchise had to be put down somewhere in a hurry for the 1960 season. Oakland was the choice. Its first coach was Eddie Erdelatz, who had done great things with the U. S. Naval Academy teams.

The Raiders played in Kezar Stadium, then in Candlestick Park, then in Youell Field, a sort of wooden-bleachers recreation area. Finally, when Wayne Valley, the hardheaded financial boss of the club, threatened to move it somewhere else, Oakland came through with its magnificent sports complex which now includes facilities for football, baseball, hockey, and basketball.

The Oakland team was a loser and a nondraw until Davis took over. He had been primarily a talent man in the background at various colleges and later for Sid Gillman, with the Los Angeles Chargers. By his own admission, all his life Davis had gotten things only by going after them but his biggest job, that of coach at Oakland, came looking for him. Said Valley: "I went looking for Al because everyone knocked him. They said he'd do anything to win. I thought it would be nice to win a little for a change."

Oakland was the AFL's second representative in the Super Bowl. It could, eventually, be the first AFL club to win one.

THE GAME: *Dallas vs. Green Bay*
THE PLACE: *Green Bay*
THE TIME: *December 31, 1967*
FINAL SCORE: *Green Bay, 21; Dallas, 17*

28. Once More, with Feeling

Dick Schaap, a widely known author and journalist, drove slowly along Green Bay's main street after a late breakfast at the Northland Hotel. He was following the crowd which was going only one way—out to Lambeau Field for the championship game between the Cowboys and the Packers. It had been pretty nippy on the way over to pick up his car, but with the heater going now it wasn't too bad.

As he passed an intersection he spotted a large thermometer meant to be read from a distance and nudged his companion. "Look at that," he said. "You'd think with the weather out here being so important the least they could do would be to fix that thermometer."

The thermometer read thirteen below zero, and it was accurate to within a degree. What wasn't accurate was the weatherman's prediction for the thirty-fifth National Football League championship game. He had estimated it would be zero at dawn, normal enough for Green Bay on the final day of the year, but that it would then climb to around fifteen at game time.

Instead it went the other way, and the switch was to make it an unforgettable day for the players, the 50,861 in the park, and the millions who watched in amazement as

Dallas and Green Bay battled under almost incredible conditions, risking frostbite along with the usual hazards of big-time football.

Everyone in Lambeau Field was there for his own particular reason. The Cowboys were seeking revenge for a last-minute loss to Green Bay in the title game the previous year. The Packers were seeking an unprecedented third straight National League crown. No one was aware of it at the time, but the Packers' head coach, Vincent Lombardi, was looking for a final victory in his field role before passing the portfolio over to his assistant, Phil Bengtson.

Dick Schaap was on hand to finish up a book on Jerry Kramer, who had been playing guard for the Packers for ten of his thirty-one years. Kramer was to provide him with a memorable finish to the book in the last thirteen seconds of the game.

Even apart from the record low temperature, the game was different from any other NFL championship contest. Beneath the turf the Green Bay management had installed eighty-five thousand dollars' worth of heating cable and other equipment. "My electric blanket," Lombardi had called it proudly. Buried six inches deep, it was supposed to keep the field soft and playable no matter what the conditions above. As it turned out, it was no match for the combination of twelve below and a fourteen-knot northwesterly breeze prepared especially for the occasion in some icebox in Alaska.

In Green Bay they dress for the occasion. Pictures of the customers that day, all of whom stuck around to the end, are memorable. Ski masks and parkas were the order of the afternoon. After it was over they went outside and wrestled with hundreds of moribund auto batteries.

The scene had been set the previous week in the first of the divisional playoffs. With sixteen teams in operation

in 1967 for the first time, the league had been split into
four sections of four teams each, instead of merely East
and West. We were placed in the "Coastal" Division along
with Los Angeles, San Francisco, and Atlanta. Draw a line
between these cities and you'll get a strange looking coast-
line.

We also had a strange finish, one I have repeatedly
maintained was unfair. We had won eleven in a row and
were the first NFL team since the 1934 Bears to get through
thirteen games without a defeat (we had been tied twice).

Los Angeles was having its best year, too, and had a
10-1-2 record coming up to our return game with them on
the West Coast. Meanwhile Green Bay, with a 9-3-1 record,
had already clinched first place in the comparatively weak
Central Division. They could even afford the indulgence
of an indifferent effort against the last-place Steelers in
their final game (the Steelers won), while the Rams and
the Colts tore each other apart for the privilege of meeting
Green Bay the following week.

Well, the Rams beat us 34–10 with one of the best pass
rushes I've been up against in a long time. That gave us
identical records: 11-1-2. Los Angeles won the divisional
title on points, and they deserved it. Nose to nose there
was no question that they were superior point-scorers. Our
first game had been a 24–24 tie, so over the season they
were two dozen points better. The Rams even scored four
more points than we did against fourteen league opponents,
but that isn't the important thing. To my way of thinking
a club with a 9-4-1 record (Green Bay) isn't as good as one
with an 11-1-2 record (we and Los Angeles). And both
Los Angeles and Baltimore had beaten Green Bay the one
time we each played them during the regular season.

We were all in the same basic Western Conference as
in previous years. What is the point of cutting it so fine?

There has to be a better system, and I have hopes that it will be straightened out when the final steps are taken in the merger of the two leagues.

Dallas got into the 1967 title game by hammering Cleveland (the Century Division winner) 52–14 in Dallas, and Green Bay pretty much neutralized the Rams' pass rush in a 28–7 victory in Milwaukee. That game projected Travis Williams, the rookie halfback from Arizona State, into national recognition. He scored two of the four Packer touchdowns that afternoon. Chuck Mercein, a reject by two Eastern clubs (New York and Washington) also took one in. Mercein was to play a vital role in the following week's championship game.

The championship game was the climax to what was perhaps the greatest year in Bart Starr's pro career. The previous season he had been named Most Valuable Player in the league. He had been intercepted only three times. In the 1967 season he was intercepted nine times in the first two games.

Everyone insisted there was nothing wrong until Lombardi revealed, on his own Wisconsin network TV show, that his quarterback was suffering from bruised ribs sustained in a preseason game and a shoulder injury picked up in the third game of the year, against Atlanta. No one ever knew whether the injuries healed by themselves or whether Bart just ignored them. He threw only nine touchdown passes (compared to fourteen the previous year), and he wound up with the highest interception percentage among regular quarterbacks, but he was still a championship leader.

As they had the previous year, the Packers scored first. In the second quarter they held a 14–0 lead on two Starr passes to Boyd Dowler, one of eight yards, the other of forty-six.

Then Dallas broke through with four minutes left in the half, and Willie Townes nailed Starr for a nineteen-yard loss. In the process Bart fumbled. George Andrie, the Dallas defensive end, picked it up and ran seven yards for a touchdown. Don Meredith's passing in the first half consisted of a mere four completions in thirteen tries, but the Cowboys hung close with a twenty-one-yard field goal by Danny Villanueva.

In the scoreless third period the Cowboys showed signs of perking up, and in the beginning of the fourth quarter a big play, a halfback pass, put the Cowboys ahead. Dan Reeves, the Cowboys' hard-working halfback, got it off to Lance Rentzel and it was good for a fifty-yard touchdown. Rentzel, the flankerback, was wide open. The Packers were completely fooled.

But with five minutes left and the title apparently slipping through their frostbitten fingers, the Packers took hold again. Their drive defied the clock and tested Starr's ability under extreme pressure.

He threw three times to Donny Anderson and once to Chuck Mercein for forty-six of the sixty-eight yards to the Dallas goal stripe. Mercein slashed through the left side for an eight-yard gain which set up the touchdown.

Anderson then picked up two yards for a first down, giving the Packers the ball on the one. There was a half-minute left and all time-outs were gone.

Starr sent Anderson into the middle again but the Dallas defense flung him back for no gain. The electric blanket had long since given up its losing fight with the elements, and it was difficult to get the traction necessary for a running play of this kind.

Anderson's attempt had consumed only ten seconds, and Starr tried the same maneuver again. This time Anderson slipped.

Green Bay obviously had time for only one more play unless they called time out and took a five-yard penalty. Starr decided to try a sneak. Jerry Kramer, the right guard, had the responsibility of clearing out the tackle just enough to let him slip through.

Jethro Pugh, Kramer's opponent, lined up on Jerry's inside shoulder. Somehow Kramer got enough of a grip with his right foot to move Pugh out of the way. The three, Starr, Kramer, and Pugh, wound up in a tight knot in the end zone. There were thirteen seconds left on the clock, enough for Meredith to try two desperation passes from deep in Dallas territory after the Packer kickoff.

When the game ended, a big, strong-looking young man visited the Green Bay dressing room. He didn't have to show any credentials at the door; he looked as though he belonged. He approached Henry Jordan, veteran of so many Packer championship teams, and said, "Mr. Jordan? I'm John Niland. I just want to tell you I really enjoyed playing against you today." Niland was Dallas's left guard. Jordan was his opposite number all afternoon.

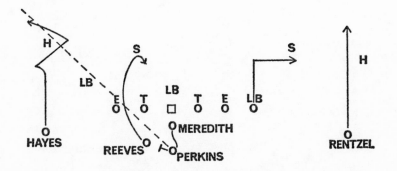

7. Typical Dallas Passing Play (Meredith to Hayes)

The defending line will rush when they read "pass" on this play.

The balding veteran and the young man looked at each other and Jordan smiled. "Thank you, John. How old are you?"

"Twenty-three," said Niland. "This is my second year in the league."

Jordan reached over and patted Niland on his broad shoulder. "Listen John," he said, "You're a good one and you got a long time ahead of you. You'll be around to win one of these championships. Maybe more than one."

"But today," Henry said, "you had to give us old-timers one more chance."

THE GAME: *Green Bay vs. Oakland*
THE PLACE: *Miami*
THE TIME: *January 14, 1968*
FINAL SCORE: *Green Bay, 33; Oakland, 14*

29. Vince's Last Hurrah

Unlike two Sundays earlier, when his Packers had won the
NFL title, Vince Lombardi was in no special hurry to get
to the dressing room after the Packers' January 1968 Super
Bowl victory. There had been hints abroad that this was
Lombardi's farewell as head coach, but only he knew this
to be true. Everyone else was guessing.

So, taking the cheers for the last time, Vince permitted
his players to give him an extra whirl around the field on
their shoulders following their well-executed victory over
the Oakland Raiders. Doing most of the shouldering were
a couple of his veteran linemen, Jerry Kramer and Forrest
Gregg. To them the two-hundred-pound Lombardi felt as
light as an eighty-five-thousand-dollar feather.

That eighty-five thousand dollars represents the estimated
"extras" a player under Lombardi's head-coaching tenure
at Green Bay had picked up from the time he drove them
to their first championship playoff against the Philadelphia
Eagles in 1960 until the second Super Bowl climax. It unquestionably made the Packers the best-paid unit in pro
football history.

The extra money came from the following:

> Super Bowls (two)
> NFL playoffs (six; five won, one lost)
> Western Conference playoffs (two)
> Conference runners-up (two)
> Playoff Bowls (two)
> Chicago All-Star games (five)

This also made the Packers the busiest ballplayers of the sixties, busy running to the bank, and busy running over the opposition, and busiest of all when responding to Lombardi's growl of "C'mere, you!"

The story is that Lombardi had to yell just once during the week before meeting Oakland, a team that had won all but one of its regular-season games in the American League. This was when the Packers, obviously tired at the end of a long year, seemed to go flat during practice in their Florida base. A few well-directed lashes from the considerable Lombardian repertory got them back on the beam.

Although their second successive Super Bowl victory wasn't the breeze the previous year's triumph over Kansas City had been, it left the master satisfied. Equally satisfied was Bart Starr, whose quarterbacking performance, despite a jammed thumb that caused him to miss two-thirds of the final period, won him another of the cars awarded by *Sport* magazine along with Most Valuable Player honors.

Starr never had to come from behind. A couple of field goals by Don Chandler and a long bomb to Boyd Dowler had given Green Bay a 13–0 edge and the customers were beginning to squirm, thinking that Super Bowl No. 2 was going to be pretty much a repetition of Super Bowl No. 1 in California a year earlier.

Dowler ran to the inside, got behind Kent McGlothan,

and took the ball with no one between him and the goal, sixty-two yards away. Not too many people have been able to catch Dowler from behind in the decade he's been in the National League.

Oakland came back with a second-period score on a pass from Daryle Lamonica to Bill Miller. Miller operated as a slotback inside Fred Biletnikoff, the flanker, and this unorthodox formation was just about the only bit of Oakland offense that bothered the Packers. The pass was good for twenty-three yards, the identical yardage this same combination picked up for a final Oakland score in the fourth period, after the Packers had all but wrapped it up.

Earlier in the fourth period Lamonica got off a weak pass to Biletnikoff. Herb Adderley, the left halfback, had no trouble stepping into it for an interception which triggered a successful sixty-yard return for six points.

Lombardi lingered in Florida for a few days of golf, saying that he still hadn't made up his mind about retiring. Then he returned to Green Bay and called a press conference a couple of days after the annual player draft.

He suggested that reporters from Green Bay and Milwaukee who covered the Packers regularly might want to have dinner with him. They could talk about his future plans, and about the Green Bay personnel for 1968. After all, Green Bay had its usual two picks in the first round of the draft, thanks to dealing off some surplus back in 1967, and the reporters might want to know about these new men.

Vince seemed surprised when more than fifty newspapermen from all over the country decided to invite themselves. They all had the feeling that if Lombardi had decided to continue as head coach he'd simply have spread the news with a phone call to the wire services. They wanted to be on hand when one of the game's few real giants announced his retirement as a coach. And they wanted to indicate an amiable skepticism about Lombardi's ability to remain a spectator when the whistle blew for the start of the next season.

14. Cookie Gilchrist off on one of his thirty-six carries in the Buffalo-New York game in 1963. He ultimately set a new record with a single-game total of 243 yards. *(UPI)*

15. This tackle by Bear linebacker Larry Morris proved costly to the Giants in the 1963 playoff. Y. A. Tittle's leg was injured on the play, and he eventually had to leave the game. The Bears proceeded to win the title. *(UPI)*

16. Here are three executioners in the 1965 "ghost game," in Baltimore, when Paul Hornung scored five times in the last big effort of his career. The customers couldn't see any of them from the stands, but the referee could. *(Courtesy of the Baltimore Colts)*

17. Gale Sayers plunges over the muddied San Francisco defenders for one of his six touchdowns during a record-setting afternoon in 1965. *(UPI)*

18. Don Chandler kicks the winning field goal in the 1965 Western Conference playoff against us in Green Bay. This one came in overtime; the one on which Chandler had tied it up late in the fourth period doesn't go through the uprights on our films. *(Wide World)*

19. Green Bay's Dave Robinson bear-hugs Dallas's Don Meredith to extinguish the Cowboys' last hope in the 1966 NFL championship. *(UPI)*

20. Max McGee had one of his finest afternoons in the first Super Bowl game, as Green Bay turned back Kansas City. Here the Packer receiver bobbles one, but manages to hold it for a touchdown. (*Wide World*)

21. Joe Namath, first man to top four thousand yards in a season, gets off a pass against Oakland in the next-to-last game of the 1967 campaign. Oakland lost but had already clinched the divisional crown. (*Courtesy of the New York Jets*)

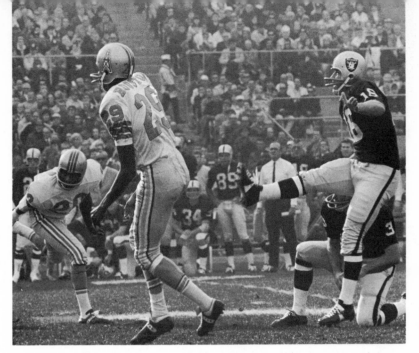

22. When the Raiders met the Oilers for the 1967 AFL title, they scored an easy victory, thanks in no small part to four successful field goals by veteran George Blanda, whom Houston had released earlier in the year. *(UPI)*

23. The coldest game in history is the way they described the Packers' 1967 title victory over the Cowboys in Green Bay. Here's proof. *(Wide World)*

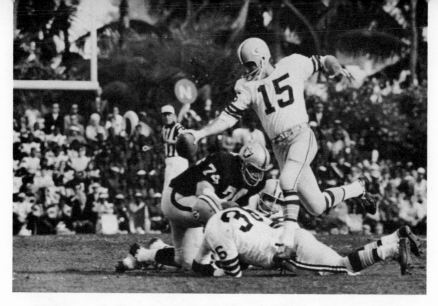

24. Two weeks later there was a drastic change in scenery. Note the palm trees serving as background for Green Bay's second Super Bowl victory, over Oakland in Miami. *(UPI)*

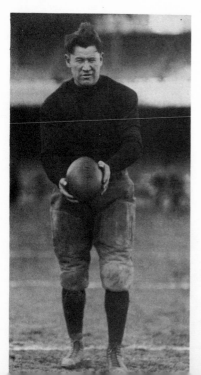

25. Jim Thorpe, regarded as the greatest athlete in the first half of the twentieth century. *(UPI)*

26. Red Grange, the famed Galloping Ghost, who did as much as anyone to popularize the pros. *(UPI)*

27. Ernie Nevers, who scored a game-record forty points with the Chicago Cardinals in the late twenties. *(UPI)*

28. Bronko Nagurski, bruising Chicago Bears' fullback, considered by many the hardest runner of them all. *(UPI)*

30. No Game for a Dummy

What's worse than being hit and dumped by some fellow weighing 270 pounds when you find all your receivers covered? Being hit and dumped by some fellow weighing 270 pounds who is not only faster than you but maybe even a little smarter. In my time in pro football I've seen a special breed of lineman develop: fast, brainy men who are twenty or thirty pounds heavier than their counterparts of the mid-fifties.

There was a time when a big strong man could just "sit in there" and take whatever came. Now they have to be smart. They have to talk to each other on the line of scrimmage in order to get the job done.

Offensively, the tackle has to talk to the guard, the guard to the center, and the center to the men on all sides to try to alert them to things that might be coming. I remember a line coach who used to get a big laugh when he became excited in a tough situation. He would call his instructions from the sideline: "Be ready for anything."

Actually that's got to be the case with linemen. If they don't talk to each other, they are bound to suffer for it. In football, unlike other fields, you can't rely on memos.

Defense is a development of the modern game. When I

first came up, there was very little strategy in that department. Everyone knew who the other fellow had to block.

If the man was right straight ahead of you, you took him no matter what the circumstances. Now it's different. Maybe the lineman might be giving something away on a particular stance, maybe the defense is tipping its hand who it is going to stunt (move from a normal defensive position). If you have a smart lineman who can pick these things up you have what amounts to an extra coach on the field.

When you talk defense you think of the rush line, the first four men a quarterback has to contend with. If they get to him the linebackers and the defensive backs can take the day off. And when you speak of a defensive line today you invariably think of the Los Angeles Rams who, in the mid-sixties, built one of the finest units in the history of the game.

They had the nucleus in Dave Jones, an end who was runner-up to me in the 1967 Most Valuable Player balloting (a remarkable tribute to a defensive lineman), Merlin Olsen at tackle, Lamar Lundy at the other end, and first Rosey Grier and then Roger Brown at the other tackle spot.

To get Rosey Grier the Rams traded John LoVetere to the Giants a few years ago. The Rams came out on top in that deal because LoVetere tore up his knee and had to retire. Then when Grier was hurt in 1967, George Allen, the Rams' coach, gave up plenty to Detroit for Roger Brown, the largest numismatist in existence (do you know of any other three-hundred-pound coin collectors?).

That entire front four has another hobby. They collect quarterbacks, or portions thereof. In mid-December of 1967, with everything riding on a Colts-Rams game (we were playing them for the Coastal Division title and the

right to meet Green Bay for the Western crown after we
had gone through thirteen games without a defeat), this
bunch dumped me a half-dozen times.

Fortunately for the opposition, a group like this comes
along only rarely. When it does people start talking about
whether the defense will ultimately overpower the offense.

Personally I don't think it will ever happen. There'll
always be a pretty good balance. One team might have a
better defense than offense, but that could be reversed a
couple of years later. You're just unlucky if you happen to
come up against a front four like the Rams have when they
all hit their peaks—and you—at once.

Just what the exact proportions of these men are is a
matter between themselves and the charts their trainer
keeps. I can tell you, though, that they're all pretty big.
If you play against a man six-seven and 280 pounds he'll
wear you down faster than a man thirty pounds lighter.
You don't have to be a genius to figure that out, especially
when the big fellow is as fast and as smart as the smaller
man. The old prize-fighting line about sums it up: "A good
big man will always beat a good little man."

The only place a "little man" has a chance in football
today is in the defensive secondary. By "little" I mean a
fellow five-ten or five-eleven. I don't think anyone under
that has much of an opportunity.

The reason the defensive secondary is the place for the
relatively small man is that he doesn't "get it" on every
play. Because of a back's shiftiness, a 250-pound guard
who comes charging out of the line has a tough job keeping
tabs on him. If a back plays his keys right he can be up
into the play before the guard gets started, and then that
250-pounder isn't nearly as tough as he is once he gets
moving. If I had to give any advice to a defensive back

it would be to get to the play before it starts upfield. It's a lot healthier.

Between the front four and the defensive secondary are the linebackers, who are a comparatively recent development in football. Originally their role was filled by ends who dropped off and a guard, or center, who pulled back. Now they represent a totally different kind of ballplayer, big enough (240-pounders aren't rare) to have been linemen and fast enough to have been backs a few years ago. Also, linebackers don't last very long unless they're thinkers.

Take Green Bay's Ray Nitschke, voted the Most Valuable Player in the 1962 playoff game. Nitschke, a balding man who wears contact lenses when he plays and is six-three and 245 pounds, has long been a mainstay of the Green Bay defense. He is a hard-nosed player, with no friends once the game starts. He yells and screams at his own personnel because he's trying to get them to hustle all the time. He's outstanding at calling the defense after diagnosing plays.

Being a fullback in college helped him in several ways. When he is watching the blocking for the opposing fullback he is quicker than most to pick up the key. They gave him a pretty good going-over when he played in the Big Ten, the same kind of punishment handed out to all ball-carriers. Now Ray is handing a little of it back, and drawing some rather handsome playoff checks for doing so.

Among defensive halfbacks, my teammate Bobby Boyd has long been a standout. Bobby was a rollout quarterback with some of those fine Oklahoma teams back in the fifties, but they never considered him for a quarterback job in the pros.

Bobby is a student of the game. He studies his man on film, trying to pick up little tips such as the way the man moves his feet or his head. His position is cornerback, which is a tough one. The safety has help from the linebackers, but the cornerback is out there sitting one-on-one with the flanker. There is no one slowing the receiver down for him.

Bobby is the leading active interception artist in the pros, although injuries in 1967 cut down his production. Even so he has a big edge on everyone else in the business. He is only five-ten and a half, and there are very few receivers to whom he doesn't give away a couple of inches.

He manages, though, and I guess it's because he's smart. I know he's smart; he went into the restaurant business with me in Baltimore in 1968.

Quarterbacks, winning quarterbacks that is, have to be smart, too. How they prepare for a game depends on each one's personality, and the same goes for the way they handle their personnel. But if they don't start off with the basic intelligence they don't last very long.

Some quarterbacks stay up all night before a game, staring at the game plan. Others have been known to stay up all night at parties, their only preparation being to shave before the game. Once they start running the show, though, they had better be the boss.

A few years ago I described my theory of quarterbacking in my life story. Basically, nothing has changed. The whole secret of football is to keep the other team off balance. If you're completely devoted to the passing game then they get ready for you that way, rushing the passer, crowding the receivers.

If you're all running, they get together tight to gang up on the blockers and smother the ball-carrier. So you have to mix 'em up. Also, you have to throw the ball sometimes when they're expecting it so that you can throw it the next time when they're *not* expecting it.

Automatics? They're made to sound very mysterious and they're supposed to make a quarterback look like a genius—picking out a flaw in the defense at the last minute and taking advantage of it.

But they're risky. Remember, you've already called a play in the huddle and the blockers have their thinking set and are ready. Now you're pulling a switch and you are asking them to forget all their preparations and take on new duties—within the space of a second or two. I've often said that by and large you're better off sticking to the play called in the huddle.

How about when you know that they're set to stop you cold, through luck or plain guessing? Well, then you have to make your decision.

The long pass, the "bomb" as it has come to be known, has always been a favorite of mine. I like it because it has a double-barreled effect if you connect . . . there's the score, of course, but you've also shaken the opposing team. There's a lot of difference between giving up a six-pointer after a long, tough drive of maybe a dozen plays with somebody finally going across from the two, and being hit with that one big throw that covers the same distance.

I'll go for the big one any time a man tells me on the way into the huddle that he can beat someone deep, or if I figure someone is playing one of our receivers a little too tight. Then again, I might throw deep even when I don't have a chance to complete it, to give the opposition something to think about. It's only one down, and I've always remembered reading somewhere that you can't make a million without risking an occasional ten-spot.

You've seen some clubs open a ball game with a half-back option pass, or something equally unorthodox. Supposing it doesn't click. Well, at least you have them thinking about it the rest of the day, waiting for something just as "nutty."

Of course, you have to follow your game plan, too. A lot of high-priced coaching talent stays up nights figuring out every possible advantage you might take over the other team, and you'd better pay attention. In the final analysis, though, it's the quarterback who does it for himself. (That's why no one talks except me once we get into the huddle.) If he isn't able to do it, they'll go get someone who can.

31. The Clock Keeps Ticking

Because championship teams invariably wind up winning more games than they lose in the last two minutes, a quarterback with championship hopes must learn how to handle himself during those last 120 seconds of play. Every major-league club practices two-minutes-to-go situations. The Colts do this once a week for twenty minutes in a simulated scrimmage. The idea is that everyone is supposed to know his job when the occasion arises.

When it does arise the quarterback shouldn't make any special emotional preparations except perhaps to steel himself to the fact that he's going to play in what amounts to an echo chamber gone wild. This type of situation brings out the loudest in the customers and you have to be able to work in spite of it. You'll never know whether it's friendly or not because all excessive noise sounds pretty much the same.

It's been said that I'm more effective in the last two minutes than at any other time, that I'm not a particularly good "front runner," that I play better when I'm behind.

Maybe these comments are justified and maybe not, but I can't subscribe to them with any particular enthusiasm. Sometimes when I find myself in one of those games-within-a-game I catch myself thinking, "If I had done my job a little better in the first fifty-eight minutes we wouldn't be needing a touchdown to win now."

There is nothing frantic about play in the last two minutes, at least not on my ball club. The Colts try to hustle it up slowly. You gain nothing and lose a lot of time overhurrying.

What happens in actual play is that the other team's defense goes into one of their special "prevent" formations to protect a lead of more than three points. Through our scouting reports and films we know what defenses they're likely to be in. Since we know these, and there are seldom more than two, we practice against them in our own "two-minutes-to-go" drills.

Every player knows what is expected of him and what he can expect from his opponent. If we get lucky and hit with a few passes against the special defense, the opposition may switch back to its original game plan. If they do, we switch back to our offensive game plan.

We don't save good scoring plays for the last couple of minutes. If a play is good we'll use it anytime. Six points are six points no matter when you put them up there on the board.

One thing we do try to do is save our three time-outs for the closing minutes of each half. If we can keep them in the bank our final effort, when it's called for, is made that much easier. Actually, we won't use these time-outs until the very last sixty seconds if everything goes well.

During the final two minutes we will use a lot of sideline passes so the receiver can step out of bounds and stop the clock. Each time the clock is stopped it stays that way until the next play begins.

The defense has been around, too, and it knows we are trying to save time, so it will play our sideline passes a little closer than normal, sometimes leaving the middle open as a result. We don't avoid the middle to save time in such situations. Instead, we use one of our time-outs when I throw a pass into the middle where the receiver can't get out of bounds. This is one of the reasons we hoard those time-outs.

In the last minute of play, when I know a time-out will be needed, I always alert the referee that I'm going to call for one as soon as the play is whistled dead. Most of the time he'll say, "I'll be looking for you." That reminder to the official helps save a second or two.

Time-outs and sideline passes eliminate most of the necessity for quick, at-the-line-of-scrimmage signals and quick-count plays. If we do get into a spot where we have to run a play while the clock is going, I will have the team line up without a huddle, call a play, and get it under way at the first count of the signal. The play will generally be a pass aimed toward the out-of-bounds line, stopping the clock and allowing a more leisurely huddle. The defense is fairly static in the last two minutes, so I seldom have to call audibles at the line of scrimmage for tactical reasons.

Whether we need a touchdown to win or whether we can do it with a field goal makes a big difference in the way we play. And the difference is caused by the manner in which the defense plays against us. If we need a touchdown to win, the defense will frequently give us the short pass, protecting against the bomb with seven defenders, and rushing with only four men.

That means I can send out five receivers instead of holding a couple back to protect me against the usual rush of the four-man line backed up by the blitz of the linebackers. What we have to worry about here is the possibility of an interception, because there are a lot of people looking for the ball.

In field-goal situations the defense will try to prevent the short pass as well as the long one. They will normally press our offense with a four-man rush and blitzing, since the short pass can put us in position to try for three points.

You can figure that we're going for the touchdown in either situation. We will take the three points if we can't get the six, but the touchdown is what we want.

Like most teams, the Colts are geared for passing in the last two minutes and will use the run only as a mixer or if the defense is such that we can take advantage of it on the ground. The reason for avoiding the run is obvious. It eats up too much time and forces us to use our time-outs. Ever notice the difference in playing time between running teams and passing teams? Well, a game relying heavily on ground attacks will finish fifteen or twenty minutes sooner than a game which has a lot of passing. That's because the clock is running not only during the play but during the huddles as well.

A passing team can take advantage of the clock in small ways, such as by picking up information from the interior linemen while the receivers are returning to the huddle. The Colt linemen will advise how their opponents are charging, either right or left, hard or soft. If the defense is coming too strong we might use a trap or a draw or a screen pass. At least we know what we can expect. When the receivers get back to the huddle they give me the dope on the defense and possible lanes of completion. Ray Berry used to be the very best at this.

When the Colts are ahead and trying to protect a slim lead we do everything possible to eat up time. I tell the backs and linemen to untangle slowly from blocks and drag back to the huddle. In the huddle I try to guess how much time we are using up. You have twenty-five seconds; if you take any more than that you will be charged with a five-yard penalty. I can't hit it on the nose but I have no trouble getting close—around twenty-three seconds all the time.

Instead of using passes when we have a small lead late in the game I call for wide sweeps to run out the clock. Getting first downs and keeping the clock running are my main concerns. A good, tough runner who can take the ball one play after another helps here.

If we do get some first downs, sooner or later the defense will have to use up its time-outs to stop the clock. Naturally, I'd much rather protect a lead than have to score with just two minutes to go.

32. Thorpe . . . Grange . . . Nevers . . . Nagurski

How far has pro football come in the last, say, quarter-century? A long way. I'll give you an example. Someone once got talking with Mel Hein, an all-pro center for the New York Giants for a dozen years and a man who is now enshrined in the Pro Football Hall of Fame in Canton, Ohio. Mel was asked, "Was there any opportunity in those days for 'outside money,' things like endorsements or appearances?"

Hein thought a while. "Well," he said, "no one paid for appearances because the only time we appeared was when *we* asked whether we could come, and it was usually to try to push some tickets. They didn't have to pay you for *that*. There weren't any endorsements, either. They wanted baseball players or polo players or skaters, or tennis players."

Mel, now supervisor of officials for the American Football League, thought a little. "Wait a minute, I remember one endorsement. It was for doughnuts. Mayflower doughnuts, and I got $150. That wasn't bad. Matter of fact, for most of the fellows that was almost a game's pay."

Needless to say, a game's pay today is a good deal more. Of course, it should be. Football is the greatest money-maker in sports. Salaries have leveled off after a half-dozen years of fierce bidding between the rival leagues. When they merged in June 1966 it wrote finish to such items as two rookies costing a top club a million-plus. As it happened, both rookies came through. Supposing both had flopped?

In the early days of pro football there weren't any flops. If you couldn't do it, they got someone else who could for the following Sunday. And if you didn't play, you didn't get paid. In today's meticulously run game the old-timers seem as distant as Indian-fighters.

But some of them, stars then, would be stars and perhaps superstars today. That includes the toughest Indian of them all, Jim Thorpe, who was voted the Athlete of the Half-Century back in the early fifties in a poll conducted by the Associated Press. Thorpe was a great natural athlete, a trackman who won Olympic championships, a baseball player, a football player. Shortly after he died they named a town in Pennyslvania after him. Mauch Chunk, Pennsylvania became Jim Thorpe, Pennsylvania, an improvement.

Thorpe took nothing out of football except Hall of Fame status. What he made during a Sunday game was spent before Sunday night had ended. Some of the early stars saved their pay, but few saw any big money.

Among those who did were Ernie Nevers and Red Grange. Grange commanded more attention, but Nevers is mentioned here first because his name is still in the record books after four decades and could well remain there a lot longer. He scored forty points (six touchdowns, four extra points) for the Chicago Cardinals against the Chicago Bears on Thanksgiving Day 1929. It was fifteen years before any *team* was able to score as many again against a George Halas club.

Nevers had a unique career. He was an all-around athlete with enough pitching talent to last for three seasons

with the St. Louis Browns. He also played pro basketball at
the time of the two-handed dribble. He began his football career as a member of the famous Duluth Eskimos,
later playing for the Chicago Cardinals. At one time someone figured he made almost as much money as did Babe
Ruth, whose paycheck equaled that of the President of the
United States.

One Nevers record not in the book, because it can't
be properly pigeonholed, has to do with the 1926 season
of the Eskimos, a NFL road club that played twenty-nine
games. Ernie played in all but twenty-seven minutes of
this amazing string. Less than half were "league" games
in this loosely knit confederation of clubs which operated
with the NFL label. Duluth finished the season with an official record of 6-5-2. Twenty-two teams were listed that
year, stretching from Providence to Los Angeles.

Duluth was the only club ever to be formally named
after a player. (The Cleveland Browns were named after
Paul Brown, their first head coach, when they began in
the All-America Conference in 1946.) The Duluth team was
known as "Ernie Nevers' Duluth Eskimos."

Fifteen players outfitted in snow-white great-coats made
quite a picture when they showed up at the depot. (NFL
player-limits in those days were fifteen minimum, eighteen maximum, and you usually played with the minimum
for maximum financial benefits to the participants.)

The split on Ernie's club was one of the more offbeat
in football history. Nevers got the big money, naturally,
because the people came to see him. At Stanford he had
been a unanimous All-America, and could do everything
with a football.

His teammates were paid on the following per-game
basis: win, seventy-five dollars; tie, sixty dollars; lose, fifty
dollars. They traveled thirteen thousand miles, coast to

coast, and averaged a game every four days between September 15 and January 5. Eventually they wound up with nineteen victories, seven losses, and three ties. They once played five games in eight days.

The Duluth franchise had an odd history. It was sold to Orange, New Jersey, then George Preston Marshall, the wet-wash king, bought it for Boston, where he installed the team as the Redskins. But Boston turned up its patrician nose at the pros, even though the Redskins won the Eastern crown. In 1937 Marshall moved the club to Washington, where it enjoyed instant success. The decline of big college football in the area had a lot to do with the way the sport caught on in Washington, that plus the spoon-fed rivalry started with the New York Giants.

As an example of how far football has come since Nevers' heydey, I'd like to quote the *entire* story carried in the newspapers the day following his memorable forty-point feat:

NEVERS DOES ALL SCORING
AS CARDS NET 40–6 VICTORY

Triumph Over Bears Gives
Winners Chicago Pro Title

CHICAGO, Nov. 28 (AP)—Ernie Nevers, former Stanford star, established an individual scoring record for one National Professional League football game today by scoring all of the Chicago Cardinals' points in their 40-to-6 victory over the Chicago Bears. Nevers drove over for six touchdowns and kicked from placement for four extra points.

The victory gave the Cards the Chicago city professional championship for the first time since 1927.

The Bears scored their only touchdown in the third period when Walt Homer passed to Garland Grange, who galloped fifty yards for the touchdown.

That was it. No lineup, no statistics, no charts, no locker-room stories or "side bars." The papers didn't have to worry about competition from TV or radio in those days. If you didn't read it in the papers you didn't know about it.

Three paragraphs, you say, and they didn't even get Red Grange's name right? Yes, they did. That "Garland" Grange was correct. He was Red's younger brother. Both came out of Illinois and both played for the Chicago Bears under George Halas.

Halas's move inducing Harold (Red) Grange to play pro ball probably did more for the game than anything up to the time Pete Rozelle convinced the owners to put their TV rights and hopes into one big pot for package sale.

Grange was a superhero in the early twenties. Big Ten ball was supreme in those days, and Grange was the best for several years, setting records on the field and styles off the field. (He worked as an iceman to keep in shape in the off-season, and every high school boy across the country promptly pestered the local iceman for an assistant's job.) Grange also wore a mohair cap with a large peak. No red-blooded young American under twenty-one would be caught dead wearing anything else.

Assisting Halas in the Grange coup was a now-forgotten figure, C. C. Pyle, a promoter years ahead of his time. Pyle ran events like a coast-to-coast professional marathon (he charged the towns for the privilege of having the runners go through—if they didn't pay he routed them around the other way) and supervised the pro tour of Suzanne Lenglen, who was quite possibly the greatest woman tennis player ever. He smelled big money in football when he read the headlines of Grange's weekly exploits, although he didn't know the laces on a football from the laces on his patent-leather shoes.

Pyle signed Grange and then found a ready audience with Halas, who was no farm boy himself. The week after the 1925 season ended, Grange turned pro. His career is one of the great chapters in the history of the game.

After Red's last college game, against Ohio State, the Bears grabbed him and showed him off in Wrigley Field to a hysterical Thanksgiving morning crowd which had come to see the Bears play their crosstown rivals, the Cardinals. They drew forty thousand. They played a couple of other games within the next week, and then took off to where additional fans were waiting to see the so-called "Galloping Ghost." This was the schedule they followed:

Saturday, Philadelphia; Sunday, New York; Tuesday, Washington; Wednesday, Boston; Thursday, Pittsburgh; Friday, Detroit; Sunday, the New York Giants back in Chicago. The game in New York drew an estimated seventy thousand. No one will ever know exactly how many saw the game. The crowd simply broke past the ticket-takers and poured in willy-nilly. The game netted $143,000, and Grange's share was thirty thousand dollars, or about one thousand dollars a minute, since he sat out an entire period wearing a coonskin coat.

Seventeen players made the trip. Halas recalled that there was some sort of three-way split arrangement among himself, Pyle, and Grange.

The Bears lived out of a Pullman car. The rest rooms at either end were used for strategy sessions and also served as training rooms and "clubhouses." Wet uniforms were strung up there each night, in the hope that they would be dry enough to be worn for the next game. If they weren't they went on, anyway.

Andy Lotshaw was the trainer and he was helped by one

of the players, Johnny Mohardt, a Notre Dame back who
became one of Chicago's leading surgeons. Working on a
lurching train proved invaluable experience for the delicate
surgery he performed in later years.

The fields on which the Bears played were, for the most
part, frozen. When they hit the ground there was no
bounce. Grange hurt his arm midway on the tour and it
had an immediate and drastic effect at the box-office. He
had to be helped off the field in Pittsburgh. In Detroit the
customers stormed the refund window when it was announced that he wasn't able to play. Back home, the Bears
took a shutout beating from the Giants and promptly swore
"never again."

This sentiment lasted just long enough for Halas and
Pyle to put together another trip. The second time they
were a lot smarter. They added a few collegiate stars, bring-
ing the squad total to twenty-two, and they stayed away
from the snow and ice. The game played in Coral Gables,
Florida, which was enjoying a real estate boom, brought
the highest price of all time for a fifty-yard box seat, $19.80.
Halas still treasures a stub from that one.

A game with an all-star team in the Coliseum in Los
Angeles drew seventy-seven thousand, which was more
than for the first Super Bowl game played there forty years
later. The Bears went up and down the West Coast
shaking the natives loose from their entertainment money
and earning the best yearly salaries the game had offered
up to that time, and for quite a while after that.

Grange played into the 1930s, and although injuries prevented him from becoming a superstar in the pros, he is a
member of the Hall of Fame. Films of Grange in action are
unfortunately of primitive quality compared to those of
today. As a result, the subtleties and nuances of Grange's
tremendous skills are lost. All we see are herky-jerky se-

quences. Change of pace, cuts, patterns, which we have come to expect on game-films are nowhere to be found in the movies of the mid-twenties and early thirties. It is a pity because Grange was unquestionably an all-time great who could have played in any era.

The same may be said of Bronko Nagurski, another Bears' Hall of Famer who had a number of distinctions, including coming back a half-dozen years after retirement to help a wartime Halas club in its drive for the 1943 title. That was thirteen years after Halas had signed him at the start of the Great Depression for the not-insignificant sum of five thousand dollars.

But then Bronko was no insignificant player. At Minnesota he had been a unanimous All-America choice as a tackle-fullback. He is alleged to be the hero of the story about the scout (allegedly the late Dr. Clarence (Fat) Spears) who interrupted a sturdy young farmer's plowing to ask for directions to the next town. The sturdy young farmer is supposed to have indicated the proper direction —using the plow for a pointer.

Bronko was six-two and 240 pounds, which would be pretty fair credentials for the role of fullback even today. In his day he was something special. Recalls a contemporary: "His stomach was as hard as a washboard, and just as rippled. And every ripple was a muscle."

It wasn't the muscles that did the damage. This came from his great, pile-driving legs, his enormous shoulders, his battering-ram neck, and his murderous enthusiasm. He had the trick of throwing a counterblock—a little dip of the shoulder before making contact with an upward thrust—that inevitably caused a rival tackler to come out a poor loser. Said a fellow who played against him through many a long afternoon: "Nagurski probably broke more shoulders than any man in football." He meant other people's shoulders.

In 1934 Beattie Feathers came out of Tennessee with an All-America reputation and signed with the Bears. He is the only man who has ever topped one thousand yards in rushing during his rookie season. (Jim Brown missed it by fifty-eight yards in his first year.)

Jim would have gone over that figure, and maybe a lot higher, had he had someone like Nagurski out in front. Nagurski's rushing record that year was half of Feathers', but everyone was aware of the importance of the second half of the combination. Feathers averaged an amazing 9.9 yards per carry, but played in only eleven of thirteen games because of injuries. (The Bears won all thirteen, incidentally, with and without him.)

Nagurski wasn't impervious to injury, but it bothered him less than most. One year he tore three ribs from their moorings and played with a special cage which was supposed to protect this area. Oddly, he managed to get away with his defiance of the general laws of nature, except that in favoring his injured side he set up a sciatica condition which made every step an agony. There was one period during which Nagurski had to be lifted to his feet by his teammates after every play. Once he was on his feet, as the opposition discovered to its intense chagrin, he was about as good as ever.

Thorpe, Grange, Nevers, Nagurski . . . Hall of Famers, all. They played, "before their time," if you consider what they received compared to what players receive today. But they were the greatest of their era. As such, they unquestionably received the best money return the game could provide at that time.

RECORDS

John Unitas

Year	Club	Games	Attempts	Completions	Pct.	Yards Gained	TD Passes	Interceptions	Avg. Gain
1956	Baltimore	12	198	110	55.6	1498	9	10	7.57
1957	Baltimore	12	301	172	57.1	2550	24	17	8.47
1958	Baltimore	10	263	136	51.7	2007	19	7	7.63
1959	Baltimore	12	367	193	52.6	2899	32	14	7.90
1960	Baltimore	12	378	190	50.3	3099	25	24	8.20
1961	Baltimore	14	420	229	54.5	2990	16	24	7.12
1962	Baltimore	14	389	222	57.1	2967	23	23	7.63
1963	Baltimore	14	410	237	57.8	3481	20	12	8.49
1964	Baltimore	14	305	158	51.8	2824	19	6	9.26
1965	Baltimore	11	282	164	58.2	2530	23	12	8.97
1966	Baltimore	14	348	195	56.0	2748	22	24	7.90
1967	Baltimore	14	436	255	58.5	3428	20	16	7.86
12-Year Totals		153	4097	2261	55.1	33,021	252	189	8.08

JOHN UNITAS' RECORD 47-GAME TOUCHDOWN STREAK

Game No.	Date	Opponent and Score	Attempts	Completions	Yardage	Interceptions	Touchdown Pass and Yardage
1.	Dec. 9, 1956	At Los Angeles, 7–31	29	14	147	1	3, to Mutscheller
2.	Dec. 16, 1956	At San Francisco, 17–30	16	11	124	1	31, to Berry
3.	Dec. 23, 1956	Washington, 19–17	18	10	161	1	53, to Mutscheller
4.	Sept. 27, 1957	Detroit, 34–14	23	14	241	3	44, to Mutscheller 35, to DuPre 35, to Berry 3, to DuPre
5.	Oct. 5, 1957	Chicago, 21–10	26	17	184	1	8, to Mutscheller 9, to Ameche
6.	Oct. 13, 1957	At Green Bay (Mil.), 45–17	17	7	130	2	12, to Mutscheller 29, to Mutscheller
7.	Oct. 20, 1957	At Detroit, 27–31	21	16	239	1	15, to Mutscheller 72, to Moore 52, to Mutscheller 4, to Moore
8.	Oct. 27, 1957	Green Bay, 21–24	31	16	188	2	52, to Berry 6, to Moore
9.	Nov. 3, 1957	Pittsburgh, 13–19	9	2	56	3	5, to Berry
10.	Nov. 10, 1957	At Washington, 21–17	30	17	247	0	67, to Berry 11, to Berry
11.	Nov. 17, 1957	At Chicago, 29–14	23	11	245	0	66, to Mutscheller
12.	Nov. 24, 1957	San Francisco, 27–21	25	16	230	0	8, to Ameche

Game No.	Date	Opponent and Score	Attempts	Completions	Yardage	Interceptions	Touchdown Pass and Yardage
13.	Dec. 1, 1957	Los Angeles, 31–14	30	18	271	1	3, to Moore 10, to Berry 50, to Moore
14.	Dec. 8, 1957	At San Francisco, 13–17	37	23	296	2	82, to Moore 2, to Moore
15.	Dec. 15, 1957	At Los Angeles, 21–37	29	14	223	2	26, to Berry
16.	Sept. 28, 1958	Detroit, 28–15	43	23	250	1	14, to Berry
17.	Oct. 4, 1958	Chicago, 51–38	23	10	198	1	12, to Berry 77, to Moore 2, to Mutscheller 33, to Moore
18.	Oct. 12, 1958	At Green Bay (Mil.), 24–17	35	16	238	1	54, to Mutscheller
19.	Oct. 19, 1958	At Detroit, 40–14	17	11	221	0	37, to Mutscheller
20.	Oct. 26, 1958	Washington, 35–10	15	8	183	0	17, to Berry 48, to Berry
21.	Nov. 2, 1958	Green Bay, 56–0	16	5	99	0	2, to Moore 5, to Ameche
—	Nov. 9, 1958	At New York, 21–24	INJURED, DID NOT PLAY				
—	Nov. 16, 1958	At Chicago, 17–0	INJURED, DID NOT PLAY				
22.	Nov. 23, 1958	Los Angeles, 34–7	18	12	218	0	58, to Moore 12, to Mutscheller
23.	Nov. 30, 1958	San Francisco, 35–27	33	17	229	1	7, to Berry
24.	Dec. 6, 1958	At Los Angeles, 28–30	38	23	214	3	3, to Berry 5, to Moore 22, to Mutscheller
25.	Dec. 14, 1958	At San Francisco, 12–21	25	11	157	0	38, to Mutscheller

Game No.	Date	Opponent and Score	Attempts	Completions	Yardage	Interceptions	Touchdown Pass and Yardage
26.	Sept. 27, 1959	Detroit, 21–9	30	13	230	0	18, to Berry 40, to Mutscheller
27.	Oct. 3, 1959	Chicago, 21–26	38	17	221	3	7, to Berry 4, to Mutscheller 13, to Mutscheller
28.	Oct. 11, 1959	At Detroit, 31–24	25	13	257	2	68, to Moore 39, to Mutscheller 53, to Berry
29.	Oct. 18, 1959	At Chicago, 21–7	30	16	233	2	25, to Moore 1, to DuPre
30.	Oct. 25, 1959	Green Bay, 38–21	29	19	206	0	8, to Berry 3, to Ameche 2, to Berry
31.	Nov. 1, 1959	Cleveland, 31–38	41	23	397	3	3, to Moore 8, to Richardson 10, to Berry 5, to Mutscheller
32.	Nov. 8, 1959	At Washington, 24–27	35	15	265	2	19, to Mutscheller 4, to Mutscheller
33.	Nov. 15, 1959	At Green Bay (Mil.), 28–24	33	19	324	0	7, to Berry 13, to Berry 24, to Mutscheller
34.	Nov. 22, 1959	San Francisco, 45–14	19	10	141	1	21, to Berry 3, to Moore
35.	Nov. 29, 1959	Los Angeles, 35–21	24	14	242	1	55, to Berry 17, to Moore

Game No.	Date	Opponent and Score	Attempts	Completions	Yardage	Inter-ceptions	Touchdown Pass and Yardage
36.	Dec. 5, 1959	At San Francisco, 35–14	36	21	273	0	7, to Berry 13, to Berry 64, to Moore
37.	Dec. 12, 1959	At Los Angeles, 45–26	27	13	110	0	7, to Berry 11, to Berry 9, to Richardson
38.	Sept. 25, 1960	Washington, 20–0	35	17	232	1	12, to Berry 66, to Moore
39.	Oct. 2, 1960	Chicago, 42–7	27	14	307	0	27, to Berry 18, to Moore 43, to Mutscheller
40.	Oct. 7, 1960	At Green Bay, 21–35	31	16	216	4	1, to Hawkins
41.	Oct. 16, 1960	Los Angeles, 31–17	23	12	176	2	22, to Moore
42.	Oct. 23, 1960	At Detroit, 17–30	40	20	253	2	22, to Berry 3, to Mutscheller
43.	Oct. 30, 1960	At Dallas, 45–7	16	8	270	0	68, to Berry 52, to Berry 70, to Berry 20, to Moore
44.	Nov. 6, 1960	Green Bay, 38–24	29	20	324	1	45, to Berry 1, to Hawkins
45.	Nov. 13, 1960	At Chicago, 24–20	33	16	266	2	21, to Berry 16, to Berry 36, to Moore 39, to Moore

Game No.	Date	Opponent and Score	Attempts	Completions	Yardage	Interceptions	Touchdown Pass and Yardage
46.	Nov. 27, 1960	San Francisco, 22–30	30	16	356	5	10, to Berry 6, to Hawkins 65, to Moore
47.	Dec. 4, 1960	Detroit, 15–20	40	22	357	3	80, to Moore 38, to Moore
	Dec. 11, 1960	At Los Angeles, 3–10	38	17	182	1	STREAK BROKEN

RECAPITULATION ON RECORD STREAK

The breakdown of figures in the forty-seven-game touchdown streak indicates seven games in which Unitas threw four touchdowns, including successive games against Dallas and Green Bay (Nos. 43 and 44). The over-all figures were thirty-one victories, sixteen losses. The streak opened at Los Angeles and closed at Los Angeles. There were six three-hundred-yard games, and they produced three victories and three losses.

There were two shutouts, including the 56-0 victory over Green Bay in which Unitas was hurt and sidelined for two games with a punctured lung.

All-time Leading Passers—Lifetime

(1500 or more attempts)

Player	Years	Atts.	Comps.	Pct.	Yards	TDs	Had Int.	Pct. Int.	Avg. Gain per Att.
1. John Unitas	12	4097	2261	55.2	33,021	252	189	4.6	8.06
2. Sonny Jurgensen	11	2792	1541	55.2	21,896	174	137	4.9	7.84
3. Bart Starr	12	2530	1443	57.0	20,009	120	108	4.3	7.91
4. Y. A. Tittle	15	3817	2118	55.5	28,339	212	221	5.8	7.42
5. Fran Tarkenton	7	2276	1228	54.0	17,667	142	114	5.0	7.76
6. Norm Van Brocklin	12	2895	1553	53.6	23,611	173	178	6.1	8.16
7. Frank Ryan	10	2062	1057	51.3	15,396	142	105	5.1	7.47
8. Otto Graham	6	1565	872	55.7	13,499	88	94	6.0	8.63
9. Sammy Baugh	16	2995	1693	56.5	21,886	186	203	6.8	7.31
10. Bill Wade	13	2523	1370	54.3	18,530	124	134	5.3	7.34
11. Sid Luckman	12	1744	904	51.8	14,683	139	130	7.5	8.42

NFL'S 10,000-YARD CLUB

(BASED ON COMBINED NET YARDAGE, INCLUDING RUSHES, PASS RECEPTIONS,
AND RUNBACKS OF INTERCEPTIONS, PUNTS, KICKOFFS, AND FUMBLES)

1. Jim Brown   15,459
2. *Bobby Mitchell   13,667
3. Ollie Matson   12,844
4. *Lenny Moore   12,451
5. *Timmy Brown   12,049
6. Hugh McElhenny   11,375
7. *Jim Taylor   10,539
8. Joe Perry   10,456
9. Jon Arnett   10,214

* Active.

Name	Position	Club and Years
Battles, Cliff	Halfback	Boston and Washington Redskins, 1932–37
Baugh, Sammy	Quarterback	Washington Redskins, 1938–52
Bednarik, Chuck	Center, linebacker	Philadelphia Eagles, 1949–62
* Bell, Bert	Owner, commissioner	Philadelphia Eagles, 1933–59
* Bidwill, Charles	Owner	Chicago Cardinals (now St. Louis), 1933–47
Brown, Paul	Head coach	Cleveland Browns, 1946–62
* Carr, Joe	Organizer-President	National League, 1920–39
* Chamberlin, Guy	Halfback, end, head coach	Canton Bulldogs, Decatur Staleys, Cleveland Bulldogs, Frankford Yellow-Jackets, Chicago Cardinals, 1919–28
Clark, Dutch	Quarterback, head coach	Portsmouth Spartans, Detroit Lions, Cleveland Rams, 1931–42
Conzelman, Jimmy	Halfback, head coach, executive	Decatur Staleys, Rock Island Independents, Milwaukee Badgers, Detroit Panthers, Providence Steam Rollers, Chicago Cardinals, 1920–48
Donovan, Art	Defensive tackle	New York Yankees, Dallas Texans, Baltimore Colts, 1950–61
Driscoll, Paddy	Halfback, head coach	Chicago Cardinals and Chicago Bears, 1919–31, and 1941–65
Dudley, Bill	Halfback	Pittsburgh Steelers, Detroit Lions, Washington Redskins, 1942, 1945–53

* No longer living.

Name	Position	Club and Years
Fortmann, Dr. Danny	Guard	Chicago Bears, 1936–46
Graham, Otto	Quarterback	Cleveland Browns, 1946–55
Grange, Red	Halfback	Chicago Bears, New York Yankees, 1925–37
Guyon, Joe	Halfback, tackle	Cleveland Indians, Oorang Indians, Rock Island Independents, Kansas City Cowboys, New York Giants, 1921–27
Halas, George	Founder, owner, end	Decatur Staleys, Chicago Bears 1920–
Healey, Ed	Tackle	Rock Island Independents, Chicago Bears, 1920–27
Hein, Mel	Center	New York Giants, 1931–45
Henry, Pete	Tackle	Canton Bulldogs, Akron Steels, New York Giants, Pottsville Maroons, Staten Island Stapletons, 1920–30
Herber, Arnie	Halfback	Green Bay Packers, New York Giants, 1930–41, 1944–45
Hinkle, Clarke	Fullback	Green Bay Packers, 1932–41
Hirsch, Elroy	End, halfback	Chicago Rockets, Los Angeles Rams, 1946–57
Hubbard, Cal	Tackle	New York Giants, Green Bay Packers, Pittsburgh Steelers, 1927–36
Hutson, Don	End	Green Bay Packers, 1935–45
* Kiesling, Walt	Guard, head coach	Duluth Eskimos, Pottsville Maroons, Boston Braves, Chicago Cardinals, Chicago Bears, Green Bay Packers, Pittsburgh Steelers, 1926–61

* No longer living.

Name	Position	Club and Years
* Lambeau, Curly	Founder, head coach, halfback	Green Bay Packers, 1919–49; Chicago Cardinals and Washington Redskins, 1950–54
Layne, Bobby	Quarterback	Chicago Bears, New York Bulldogs, Detroit Lions, Pittsburgh Steelers, 1948–62
Luckman, Sid	Quarterback	Chicago Bears, 1939–50
Lyman, Link	Tackle	Canton Bulldogs, Cleveland Bulldogs, Chicago Bears, 1922–34
* Mara, Tim	Founder	New York Giants, 1925–
Marshall, George	Founder	Boston and Washington Redskins, 1932–
McAfee, George	Halfback	Chicago Bears, 1940–41, 1945–50
McNally, John (Blood)	Halfback	Milwaukee Badgers, Duluth Eskimos, Pottsville Maroons, Green Bay Packers, Pittsburgh Steelers, 1925–39
Michalske, Mike	Guard	New York Yankees and and Green Bay Packers, 1927–37
Millner, Wayne	End	Boston and Washington Redskins, 1936–41
Motley, Marion	Fullback	Cleveland Browns, Pittsburgh Steelers, 1946–53, 1955
Nagurski, Bronko	Fullback, tackle	Chicago Bears, 1930–37, 1943
Nevers, Ernie	Fullback, head coach	Duluth Eskimos and Chicago Cardinals, 1926–31, 1939
* Owen, Steve	Tackle, head coach	Kansas City Cowboys, New York Giants, 1924–53
* Ray, Hugh (Shorty)	Technical adviser, officials' supervisor	National League, 1938–56
Reeves, Dan	Founder	Los Angeles Rams, 1945–
Rooney, Art	Founder	Pittsburgh Steelers, 1933–

* No longer living.

Name	Position	Club and Years
Strong, Ken	Halfback, kicker	Staten Island Stapletons, New York Giants, New York Yankees (AAC), 1929–37, 1944–47
Stydahar, Joe	Tackle	Chicago Bears, 1936–42, 1945–46
Thorpe, Jim	Halfback	Canton Bulldogs, Pine Village A.A., Oorang Indians, Toledo Maroons, Rock Island Independents, New York Giants, 1915–26
Trafton, George	Center	Chicago Bears, 1920–32
Trippi, Charlie	Halfback, quarterback	Chicago Cardinals, 1947–55
Tunnell, Emlen	Halfback	New York Giants, Green Bay Packers, 1948–61
Turner, Clyde (Bulldog)	Center	Chicago Bears, 1940–52
Van Buren, Steve	Halfback	Philadelphia Eagles, 1944–51
Waterfield, Bob	Quarterback	Cleveland and Los Angeles Rams, 1945–52
Wojciechowicz, Alex	Center, linebacker	Detroit Lions, Philadelphia Eagles, 1938–50

Year	Player and Club	Games	Yards
1934	Beattie Feathers (R), Chicago Bears	13	1004
1947	Spec Sanders, New York Yankees	14	1432
	Steve Van Buren, Philadelphia Eagles	12	1008
1949	Steve Van Buren, Philadelphia Eagles	12	1146
	Tony Canadeo, Green Bay Packers	12	1052
1953	Joe Perry, San Francisco 49ers	12	1018
1954	Joe Perry, San Francisco 49ers	12	1049
1956	Rick Casares, Chicago Bears	12	1126
1958	Jim Brown, Cleveland Browns	12	1527
1959	Jim Brown, Cleveland Browns	12	1329
	J. D. Smith, San Francisco 49ers	12	1036
1960	Jim Brown, Cleveland Browns	12	1257
	Jim Taylor, Green Bay Packers	12	1101
	John David Crow, St. Louis Cardinals	12	1011
1961	Jim Brown, Cleveland Browns	14	1408
	Jim Taylor, Green Bay Packers	14	1307
1962	Jim Taylor, Green Bay Packers	14	1474
	John Henry Johnson, Pittsburgh Steelers	14	1141
	Cookie Gilchrist, Buffalo Bills	14	1096
	Abner Haynes, Dallas Texans	14	1049
	Dick Bass, Los Angeles Rams	14	1033
	Charlie Tolar, Houston Oilers	14	1012
1963	* Jim Brown, Cleveland Browns	14	1863
	Clem Daniels, Oakland Raiders	14	1099
	Jim Taylor, Green Bay Packers	14	1018
	Paul Lowe, San Diego Chargers	14	1010
1964	Jim Brown, Cleveland Browns	14	1446
	Jim Taylor, Green Bay Packers	14	1169
	John Henry Johnson, Pittsburgh Steelers	14	1048
1965	Paul Lowe, San Diego Chargers	14	1121
	Jim Brown, Cleveland Browns	14	1544
1966	Gale Sayers, Chicago Bears	14	1231
	Leroy Kelly, Cleveland Browns	14	1141
	Dick Bass, Los Angeles Rams	14	1090
	† Jim Nance, Boston Patriots	14	1458
1967	Leroy Kelly, Cleveland Browns	14	1205
	Jim Nance, Boston Patriots	14	1216
	Hoyle Granger, Houston Oilers	14	1194
	Mike Garrett, Kansas City Chiefs	14	1087

(R) *Rookie*
* *NFL record*
† *AFL record*

PASS RECEIVING

1200 YARDS OR MORE, ONE SEASON

Name and Club	Year	Total Yards Gained	Total Receptions	Average No. of Yards Per Reception
Charley Hennigan, Houston (AFL)	1961	1746	82	21.3
Lance Alworth, San Diego (AFL)	1965	1602	69	23.2
Charley Hennigan, Houston (AFL)	1964	1561	101	15.4
(a) Elroy Hirsch, Los Angeles (NFL)	1951	1495	66	22.7
Bill Groman, Houston (AFL)	1960	1473	72	20.5
Bobby Mitchell, Washington (NFL)	1963	1436	69	20.8
Don Maynard, New York (AFL)	1967	1434	71	20.2
Bobby Mitchell, Washington (NFL)	1962	1384	72	19.2
Lance Alworth, San Diego (AFL)	1966	1383	73	18.9
Art Powell, Oakland (AFL)	1964	1361	76	17.9
Dave Parks, San Francisco (NFL)	1965	1344	80	16.8
Art Powell, Oakland (AFL)	1963	1304	73	17.9
(a) Ray Berry, Baltimore (NFL)	1960	1298	74	17.5
Otis Taylor, Kansas City (AFL)	1966	1297	58	22.4
Buddy Dial, Pittsburgh (NFL)	1963	1295	60	21.6
Pat Studstill, Detroit (NFL)	1966	1266	67	18.9
Don Maynard, New York (AFL)	1960	1265	72	17.6
Ben Hawkins, Philadelphia (NFL)	1967	1265	59	21.4
Lionel Taylor, Denver (AFL)	1960	1235	92	13.4
Lance Alworth, San Diego (AFL)	1964	1235	61	20.2
Bob Hayes, Dallas (NFL)	1966	1232	64	19.3
(a) Bill Howton, Green Bay (NFL)	1952	1231	53	23.2
Don Maynard, New York (AFL)	1965	1218	68	17.9
(a) Bob Boyd, Los Angeles (NFL)	1954	1212	53	22.9
(b) Don Hutson, Green Bay (NFL)	1942	1211	74	16.4
Lance Alworth, San Diego (AFL)	1963	1206	61	19.8
Jackie Smith, St. Louis (NFL)	1967	1205	56	21.5
Johnny Morris, Chicago (NFL)	1964	1200	93	12.9

(a) *12-game season*
(b) *11-game season*
All others, 14-game season

Top All-time Scoring Performances

Pos.	Name and Team	Year	TDs	Pts. after TD	Field Goals	Total
1.	Paul Hornung, Green Bay	1960	15	41	15	176
2.	Gino Cappelletti, Boston	1964	7	37	25	155
3.	Gino Cappelletti, Boston	1961	8	48	17	147
4.	Paul Hornung, Green Bay	1961	10	41	15	146
5.	Don Hutson, Green Bay	1942	17	33	1	138
6.	Gene Mingo, Denver	1962	4	32	27	137
7.	Gale Sayers, Chicago	1965	22	0	0	132
8.	Gino Cappelletti, Boston	1965	9	27	17	132
9.	Gino Cappelletti, Boston	1962	5	38	20	128
	Doak Walker, Detroit	1950	11	38	8	128
	Cookie Gilchrist, Buffalo	1962	15	14	8	128

ALL-TIME INDIVIDUAL STARS

RUSHING

JIM BROWN

Year	Team	Games	Attempts	Yards Gained	Avg. Gain	Long Gain	TDs
1957	Cleveland	12	202	942	4.7	69	9
1958	Cleveland	12	257	1527	5.9	65	17
1959	Cleveland	12	290	1329	4.6	70	14
1960	Cleveland	12	215	1257	5.8	71	9
1961	Cleveland	14	305	1408	4.6	38	8
1962	Cleveland	14	230	996	4.3	31	13
1963	Cleveland	14	291	1863	6.4	80	12
1964	Cleveland	14	280	1446	5.2	71	7
1965	Cleveland	14	289	1544	5.3	67	17
9-Year Totals		118	2359	12,312	5.2	80	106

Pass Receiving

Raymond Berry

Year	Club	Games	Passes Caught	Yards	Average Gain in Yards	TDs
1955	Baltimore	12	13	205	15.8	0
1956	Baltimore	12	37	601	16.2	2
1957	Baltimore	12	47	800	17.0	6
1958	Baltimore	12	56	794	14.2	9
1959	Baltimore	12	66	959	14.5	14
1960	Baltimore	12	74	1298	17.5	10
1961	Baltimore	12	75	873	11.6	0
1962	Baltimore	14	51	687	13.5	3
1963	Baltimore	9	44	703	16.0	3
1964	Baltimore	12	43	663	15.4	6
1965	Baltimore	14	58	739	12.7	7
1966	Baltimore	14	56	786	14.0	7
1967	Baltimore	6	11	167	15.2	1
13-Year Totals		153	631	9275	14.8	68

LOU GROZA

Year	Club	Touchdowns	Extra Points Attempted	Extra Points Made	Field Goals Attempted	Field Goals Made	Total Points
1946	Cleveland (AAC)	0	47	45	29	13	84
1947	Cleveland (AAC)	0	42	39	19	7	60
1948	Cleveland (AAC)	0	52	51	19	8	75
1949	Cleveland (AAC)	0	35	34	9	2	40
4-Year AAC Totals		0	176	169	76	30	259
1950	Cleveland (NFL)	1	29	29	19	13	74
1951	Cleveland (NFL)	0	43	43	23	10	73
1952	Cleveland (NFL)	0	32	32	33	19	89
1953	Cleveland (NFL)	0	40	39	26	23	108
1954	Cleveland (NFL)	0	38	37	24	16	85
1955	Cleveland (NFL)	0	45	44	22	11	77
1956	Cleveland (NFL)	0	19	18	20	11	51
1957	Cleveland (NFL)	0	32	32	22	15	77
1958	Cleveland (NFL)	0	38	36	19	8	60
1959	Cleveland (NFL)	0	37	33	16	5	48
1960	Inactive as player, served as scout.						
1961	Cleveland (NFL)	0	38	37	23	16	85
1962	Cleveland (NFL)	0	35	33	30	14	75
1963	Cleveland (NFL)	0	43	40	23	15	85

Year	Club	Touchdowns	Extra Points Attempted	Extra Points Made	Field Goals Attempted	Field Goals Made	Total Points
1964	Cleveland (NFL)	0	50	49	33	22	115
1965	Cleveland (NFL)	0	45	45	25	16	93
1966	Cleveland (NFL)	0	52	51	23	9	78
1967	Cleveland (NFL)	0	43	43	12	11	76
17-Year NFL Totals		1	659	641	393	234	1349
21-Year Career Totals		1	835	810	469	264	1608

Pass Receiving, Touchdowns

DON HUTSON

Year	Club	Games	Passes Caught	Yards	Average Gain in Yards	TDs
1935	Green Bay	10	18	420	23.3	6
1936	Green Bay	12	34	536	15.8	9
1937	Green Bay	11	41	552	13.5	7
1938	Green Bay	10	32	548	17.1	9
1939	Green Bay	11	34	846	24.9	6
1940	Green Bay	11	45	664	14.8	7
1941	Green Bay	11	58	738	12.7	10
1942	Green Bay	11	74	1211	16.4	17
1943	Green Bay	10	47	776	16.5	11
1944	Green Bay	10	58	866	14.9	9
1945	Green Bay	10	47	834	17.7	9
11-Year Totals		117	488	7991	16.4	100*

* Scored 1 TD rushing and 1 TD on an interception for total of 102.

INTERCEPTIONS

EMLEN TUNNELL

Year	Club	Games	Interceptions	Yards	Average Gain in Yards	TDs
1948	New York Giants	8	7	116	16.6	1
1949	New York Giants	12	10	251	25.1	2
1950	New York Giants	12	7	167	23.9	0
1951	New York Giants	12	9	74	8.2	0
1952	New York Giants	12	7	149	21.3	0
1953	New York Giants	12	6	117	19.5	0
1954	New York Giants	12	8	108	13.5	0
1955	New York Giants	12	7	76	10.9	0
1956	New York Giants	12	6	87	14.5	0
1957	New York Giants	12	6	87	14.5	1
1958	New York Giants	12	1	8	8.0	0
1959	Green Bay	12	2	20	10.0	0
1960	Green Bay	12	3	22	7.3	0
1961	Green Bay	13	0	0	0	0
14-Year Totals		165	79	1282	16.2	4

PUNT RETURNS

EMLEN TUNNELL

Year	Club	Games	Punt Returns	Yards	Average Gain in Yards	TDs
1948	New York Giants	8	12	115	9.6	0
1949	New York Giants	12	26	315	12.1	1
1950	New York Giants	12	31	305	9.8	0
1951	New York Giants	12	34	489	14.4	3
1952	New York Giants	12	30	411	13.7	0
1953	New York Giants	12	38	223	5.9	0
1954	New York Giants	12	21	70	3.3	0
1955	New York Giants	12	25	98	3.9	1
1956	New York Giants	12	22	120	5.5	0
1957	New York Giants	12	12	60	5.0	0
1958	New York Giants	12	6	0	0.0	0
1959	Green Bay	12	1	3	3.0	0
1960	Green Bay	12	0	0	0	0
1961	Green Bay	13	0	0	0	0
14-Year Totals		165	258	2209	8.6	5

Kickoff Returns

ABE WOODSON

Year	Club	Games	Kickoff Returns	Yards	Average Gain in Yards	TDs
1958	San Francisco	9	11	239	21.7	0
1959	San Francisco	12	13	382	29.4	1
1960	San Francisco	12	17	498	29.3	0
1961	San Francisco	14	27	782	29.0	1
1962	San Francisco	14	37	1157	31.3	0
1963	San Francisco	14	29	935	32.2	3
1964	San Francisco	14	32	880	27.5	0
1965	St. Louis	13	27	665	24.6	0
1966	St. Louis	14	0	0	0	0
9-Year Totals		116	193	5538	28.7	5

Ever since he was in grammar school, JOHN UNITAS knew he wanted to be a professional football player. In his senior year in high school he was quarterback on the All-Catholic High School Team and received honorable mention for the All-America High School Team. He attended the University of Louisville on a football scholarship, and after graduation was drafted by the Pittsburgh Steelers. Dropped from the squad before the season began, he took a heavy construction job and played semi-pro football for six dollars a game. The following season he joined the Colts, with whom he has played for the last dozen years, becoming the highest-paid performer in the game today. His is one of the great success stories in American sports, a success which traces to a blending of ability, character, and leadership, virtues as old-fashioned as the high-top playing shoes he wears, but equally helpful.

HAROLD ROSENTHAL began covering pro football for the New York *Herald Tribune* in the 1930s and was still on the pro "beat" when that famous newspaper stopped its presses forever in the spring of 1966. He has since been engaged in football front-office and public relations work. A former president of the Football Writers Association and a director of the New York chapter of the Baseball Writers Association, his previous books include *Baseball Is Their Business, Baseball's Best Managers,* and *The Big Play.* He is currently editorial director of Maco Publications' football magazines, *Sports All-Stars Football* and *All-Pro Football.*